Welcome to the World of Leadership

Definition of Leadership:
***Leadership** is the ability to lead yourself and/or others. Leadership combines thinking of ideas and putting ideas into practice.*

LEAD YOURSELF

LEAD OTHERS

Believe in Yourself and Your Abilities to Conduct Leadership Training Programs

Exert your own leadership to make this program the best program for you and your students. Use all or part of this program. Or, use this program as a starting point for developing your own Leadership training program. You can do it. Be a role model of tolerance, respect for all participants, good emotional balance, risk-taking, knowledge and skills.

Believe in your abilities to lead yourself and others.

Leadership Publishers Inc.
Books, Workshops, Seminars
Post Office Box 8358
Des Moines, IA 50301

Lois F. Roets
Lois F. Roets Ed.D.

Leadership: A Skills Training Program, Ages 8-18

Author: **Lois F. Roets** *Ed.D.*

Table of Contents

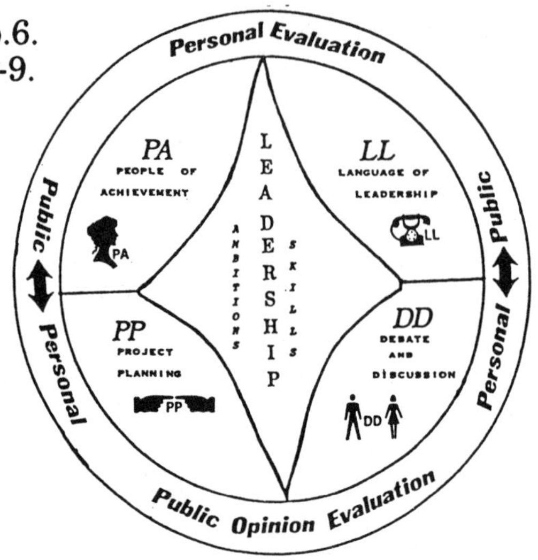

8th edition

ISBN: 0-911943-52-8

First public information sharing on ROETS LEADERSHIP TRAINING PROGRAM

AMERICAN ASSOCIATION OF SCHOOL ADMINISTRATORS NEWSLETTER APRIL, 1982

LEADERSHIP TRAINING, OR SERENDIPITY IN IOWA

Leadership is a necessary skill in rural America, Lois Roets, a coordinator of the talented/gifted program in the North Mahaska Schools at New Sharon, Iowa, believes. The same person, she points out, may serve on school and church committees, sit on the town council and be actively involved in decisions on local improvements. Such opportunities to lead, she decided, needed young people prepared for them. Consequently, she developed a leadership training program for elementary schools that has expanded to high schools, been requested by the adults in the community for themsleves and being held up as a model throughout Iowa. Quite an accomplishment to come out of a 560-student school system, where the main interest is in hog, beef and grain farming!

The program has five parts:

* The study of persons of achievement, to broaden students' awareness of people who have tried and succeeded and who can be role models for them. The study covers inventors, improvers of transportation, writers and a special category of "People Driven by Strong Convictions," such as Martin Luther King, Jr., Clara Barton and Carrie Nation.

* The language of leadership. Skills taught and practiced in this phase include reading facial expressions, body language, use of symbols, practicing social phrases of courtesy and inquiry, public speaking, impromptu statements of persuasion, ways to discourage and encourage a speaker, listening skills and different ways of responding to situations. These skills are learned through direct instruction, brainstorming techniques, drama and roleplaying. According to Roets, the skill that makes the most difference in the students is public speaking, especially knowing how to be prepared and to sound convincing.

* Project planning. Students learn how to put an idea into reality. "Some students have marvelous ideas, but lack the ability to visualize what events should take place," she says. "Other students can see what needs to be done but have a difficult time sharing that plan with others." Still others have trouble getting an idea into focus. Students learn how to "visualize," to picture a process or a product. They progress to listing the materials needed, planning and an understanding of "lead, follow or get out of the way" on projects.

* Discussion. This is a "catch all" for issues pertinent to the local school and students. It covers such issues as local problems, peer pressures and cooperation with parents and school administration.

* Evaluation. Students give opinions on the program, both in a group and individually, written and in an interview.

This leadership training program began as a K-6 project, in 10-hour sessions held during the summer. It was so popular with parents and the community that an advanced version was written for students in grades 7-12. To date, says Roets, about 14% of the students in the school district have completed the program, all on their own time during the summer or on Saturdays. By request of adults in the community, an adult version is being taught at night. Teachers throughout the state are being trained to use it, primarily through sessions by regional education agencies.

"This leadership training program has been good for our students and community," reports Roets. "It has brought attention to a needed area of instruction. It has formed a bond among those students who have completed the program. And it has helped put our talented and gifted program on a firm foundation." It is a way, she says, to show that a program can enrich the lives of not only students, but of an entire community.

"If you don't run your life, somebody else will."
— John Atkinson, educator

Persons of Achievement serve as role models for us. People who have achieved something of significance, inspire us and help us to see our own need to achieve as something that is noble, desirable and possible.

In this part of the LEADERSHIP program, several groups of persons will be studied. We will study inventors, men and women of letters, persons of strong convictions.

Let men and women of achievement become part of your thinking. Let them inspire you and encourage you.

"You don't die in the United States. You underachieve."
— Jerry Kosinski

PA 1

People of Achievement shape our world.
People of Achievement:

- √ invent something new,
- √ add to something to make it better,
- √ add new and better ways to do things,
- √ make the world a safer and healthier place, and
- √ promote causes.

Directions: Some areas of achievement that need improvement are listed below. Read these suggestions. Add your own suggestions in the open boxes.

WANTED

Leadership in Many Areas

PEACE

PA 2

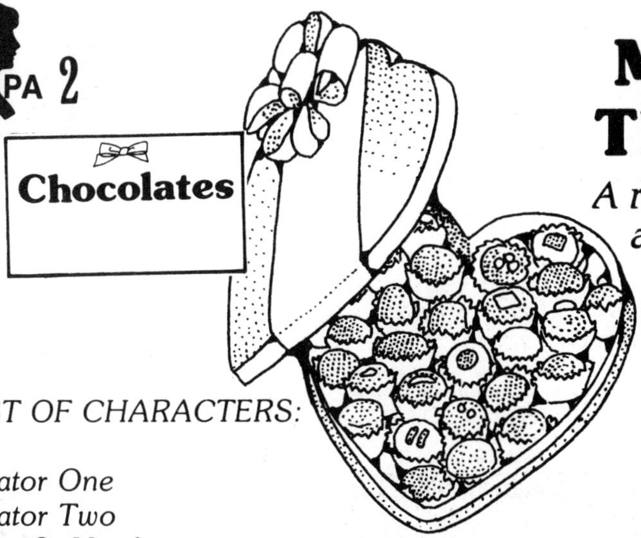

Milton S. Hershey: The Chocolate King

A reader's theatre presentation on the life and achievements of Milton Hershey.

CAST OF CHARACTERS:

Narrator One
Narrator Two
Milton S. Hershey
Milton's Mother
Milton's Aunt Mattie
Sam Ernst, newspaper publisher

NARRATOR ONE: Can you imagine a world without the yummy, velvety taste of milk chocolate? Can you imagine a world with no Hershey® bars? Can you imagine a world that didn't have a little Hershey's Kiss®?

NARRATOR TWO: Milk chocolate delights did not exist when Milton S. Hershey was born in 1857 to a family farm near Harrisburg, Pennsylvania. The parents took their farm produce to cities to sell it at open markets. On these Saturdays, Milton helped the family. He liked to visit the candy store, or confectionery shop, as it was then called.

NARRATOR ONE: At age 14, Milton Hershey's formal education ended. He was apprenticed to Sam Ernst, a newspaper editor and publisher.

NARRATOR TWO: Sam Ernst was a short-tempered man. And Milton Hershey didn't like, nor seemed fitted to, the newspaper work.

ERNST: I will accept you as my apprentice. I expect you here early in the morning. If there is work to be done, you will stay late in the evening.

HERSHEY: Yes, Mr. Ernst.

ERNST: My newspaper is published once a week. So, on some days, when we are not so busy here in the print shop, you will do chores on the farm.

HERSHEY: Yes, Mr. Ernst.

ERNST: I will show you how to set type and how to run the printing presses.

HERSHEY: Yes, Mr. Ernst.

NARRATOR ONE: But Milton Hershey had never liked school too much. And setting type, which demanded much reading and spelling, was not to his liking.

NARRATOR TWO: Sam Ernst fired Hershey when he accidently dropped a tray of letters onto the floor, and accidentally dropped his straw hat into an operating printing press!

ERNST: You're fired! Don't ever come back!

HERSHEY: Yes, Mr. Ernst.

NARRATOR ONE: Milton was relieved that he did not have to go back to the shop. His father was disappointed.

NARRATOR TWO: Milton's father wanted Milton to go back to the print shop. But his mother and Aunt Mattie had other ideas.

AUNT MATTIE: I hear that Royer's candy and ice cream shop needs a boy to learn the trade and to help with other shop tasks.

HERSHEY: A candy and ice cream business! Great! I'd like to work there.

MOTHER: I heard about that job the other day as I was shopping. Milton's father and I discussed the possibility of Milton working there. But Milton's father doesn't think that making candy is a suitable occupation for a man.

AUNT MATTIE: Nonsense. Candy and sweets are some of life's delights. The candy business can be a man's or woman's occupation. Besides, Milton has lost his job, and he is not one for more schooling. He had better learn another trade.

NARRATOR ONE: Aunt Mattie always did believe in Milton. Her support and understanding always helped Milton. Her ideas helped Milton get the job at Royer's candy shop.

NARRATOR TWO: And so it was settled. Milton went to work at Royer's confectionary and ice cream shop.

AUNT MATTIE: How was your work today, Milton?

HERSHEY: Just grand. Today I started to decorate cakes. I think I will be a good cake decorator. I have already learned how to make ice cream and some of the candies. He has put me in charge of roasting some of the peanuts and other nuts. I must still learn more about taffy. Taffy is a challenge.

AUNT MATTIE: And why is taffy a challenge?

HERSHEY: Taffy is a challenge because if you cook the mixture too much or not enough, the mixture cannot be pulled into smooth delicious taffy.

MOTHER: I'm so happy you like your work.

AUNT MATTIE: Of course, he likes his work. A person has to work where the work is suited to his abilities and interests.

MOTHER: Sometimes we must do work we don't like.

AUNT MATTIE: That is true for many of one's daily tasks, but should not be true of one's real work. Our Milton knows what he likes, and that is the candy making process.

NARRATOR ONE: After four years at Royer's confectionery shop, Milton was ready to go into business for himself. He was 19 years of age when he started his first business.

HERSHEY: It's time I go into business for myself. I have learned all I can from others.

MOTHER: Running a business takes money. And it takes a good product that people will buy over and over again.

HERSHEY: I make good candies. I've saved some money.

MOTHER: I'll help you.

AUNT MATTIE: Your candies are delicious. And I've saved some money that you may have.

NARRATOR ONE: Milton Hershey started his own business. His first business sold "penny candies" to neighborhood children. He also sold decorated cakes, fruits, nuts and special candies.

NARRATOR TWO: One cannot get rich and buy new equipment on "penny candies" and small orders of cakes, nuts and fruits. His money soon gave out. His first business had failed.

NARRATOR ONE: Milton S. Hershey had several other unsuccessful business ventures. His mother and Aunt Mattie did stay with him, lent him their money, and spent many hours helping Milton with his business.

NARRATOR TWO: Then Milton tried another candy business. He borrowed money and manufactured caramels. He used a special recipe for the caramels, adding milk to the other ingredients. The milk gave the caramels a special smooth, delicious taste. His mother and Aunt Mattie wrapped the caramels.

MOTHER: I'm happy I can help Milton wrap his candies. His business is succeeding.

AUNT MATTIE: I knew our Milton was not a failure. He is a great success.

MOTHER: Milton tells me that he should begin specializing in something other than caramels. He thinks caramels are a passing fad. He is thinking of making a better-tasting chocolate candy.

AUNT MATTIE: Will he sell his caramel business if he goes into the chocolate business?

MOTHER: I'm not sure. Neither is Milton.

AUNT MATTIE: Chocolate may be better than caramels. Chocolate candy can be made into so many different varieties and kinds. Milton may wish to specialize in chocolate.

MOTHER: Oh, Aunt Mattie. You and Milton both seem to have so many ideas.

AUNT MATTIE: To me, your son is like a son, business partner and friend, all put into one young man. Milton Hershey may become the Chocolate King of Chocolate Candies.

NARRATOR ONE: Aunt Mattie was right. Milton Hershey sold his caramel business in 1900 for $1,000,000. Today, one million dollars will buy many things. In 1900, it would buy many more things. After he sold his caramel business, he put all his energies and money into developing a better chocolate product.

NARRATOR TWO: Milton did go on to develop a better chocolate product. He invented a process of adding milk to the chocolate. This gave the chocolate a velvety smooth taste and texture. He made milk chocolate candies into many shapes and varieties.

NARRATOR ONE: Milton Hershey had many successes and failures in life. His milk chocolates had become one of his greatest successes, and the world's delight.

NARRATOR TWO: Milton S. Hershey had become the Chocolate King of the World.

HERSHEY: Yes, I am called the Chocolate King. Eat my candies and give my chocolate kisses to those you love. Come see Hershey, Pennsylvania, a city I planned and developed.

Believe in yourself and lead yourself. When the time is right, lead others. Set your goals, and work very hard to achieve those goals.

When you are feeling frustrated, give yourself a little Hershey's kiss. Share a milk chocolate treat with your friends.

Smile . . . and . . . get back to work!

The End

Discussion questions:

1. *In what way(s) was Hershey a leader?*
2. *How did Hershey lead himself?*
3. *Discuss this statement: To succeed in business you must have:*
   - a. *a product or service customers will buy,*
   - b. *money to get started,*
   - c. *"legwork" or sales approach that brings the product to the attention of the customers.*
4. *What would you like to invent that could make the world a happier place?*

PA 3

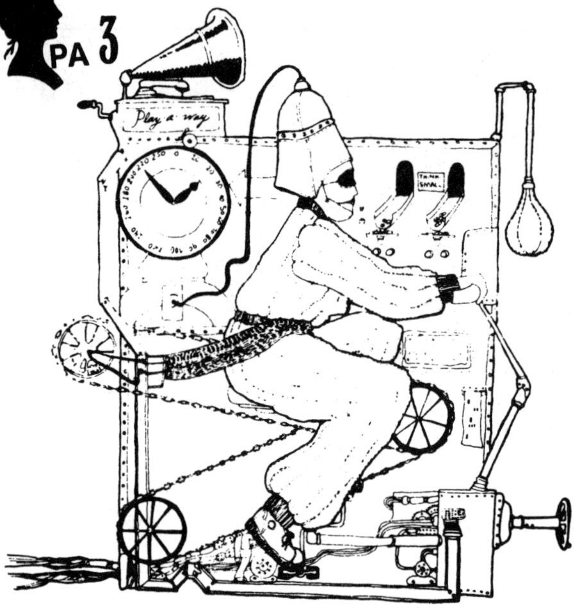

Inventors

> *"As long as fashion, instead of good common sense, continues to dictate the choice of footwear, we'll be in business."*
>
> *— Dr. William Scholl*

Category INVENTORS

THIS GROUP OF PEOPLE IS IMPORTANT BECAUSE:

Inventors try to make life easier for themselves and for others. They see needs and desires.

Directions: Match the inventor with the invention.

Alexander Graham Bell	Galileo	Walter Hunt	Cyrus H. McCormick
Clarence Birdseye	King C. Gillette	Whitcomb L. Judson	Samuel F. B. Morse
Samuel Colt	Joseph H. Glidden	Edwin H. Land	Lewis E. Waterman
Thomas Edison	Johannes Gutenberg	Hans Lippershey	Eli Whitney

Barbed wire ______________________

Cotton gin ______________________

Fountain pen ______________________

Frozen food process ______________________

Incandescent light ______________________

Polaroid camera ______________________

Printing with movable type ______________________

Reaper ______________________

Revolver (repeating) ______________________

Safety pin ______________________

Safety razor ______________________

Telegraph (electric) ______________________

Telephone ______________________

Telescope ______________________

Thermometer ______________________

Zipper ______________________

INVENTORS and INVENTIONS

1. Make a list of inventions you think would make the world a better place in which to live.

2. Make a list of inventions that you think you could invent.

3. List inventions that you think significantly changed the world. These can be from ages past or recent history.

Suggestion: The books of Jules Verne could be arranged on a table in front of the readers theater group. The titles of the books, and a brief summary of each, could be reviewed before and/or after the reading.

5 PA

Jules Verne: Prophet of Our Future

A readers' theater presentation on the life and writings of Jules Verne.

Characters:

Narrator One

Narrator Two

Dr. Ferguson, captain of the Victoria, a balloon that flew over Africa. Dr. Ferguson is from Verne's book FIVE WEEKS IN A BALLOON.

Captain Nemo, captain of the submarine, the NAUTILUS. Captain Nemo is from the book TWENTY THOUSAND LEAGUES UNDER THE SEA.

NARRATOR ONE: The subject for today's theater is Jules Verne, the French novelist who lived from 1828 to 1905. Some of his stories are: **AROUND THE WORLD IN EIGHTY DAYS, TWENTY THOUSAND LEAGUES UNDER THE SEA, JOURNEY FROM THE EARTH TO THE MOON, FIVE WEEKS IN A BALLOON** and other stories which combined science, geography and exploration.

NARRATOR TWO: Jules Verne is a special kind of leader - a writer. A writer leads self by getting ideas then completing the work of writing and rewriting. A writer is also a leader because he can inform, persuade, and spark ideas in others.

NARRATOR ONE: Jules Verne, the author and leader we are honoring, always wondered what was beyond his home town. His father wanted him to become a lawyer. Jules could not get interested in law.

To please his father, Jules went to Paris to study law but he wanted to be a writer. He lived in a very small room that was often very cold. To stay warm, he went to the library. It was warm and bright in the library. It was in the library that Jules Verne began to read every geography and science book he could find. He took notes on all his readings.

NARRATOR TWO: Jules Verne held many jobs but none interested him. He escaped the real world by reading and remembering everything that he had read. He wanted to write but it is difficult to earn a living as a writer.

After many unsuccessful jobs and rejected manuscripts, Verne wrote about a balloon. That story of the balloon was the turning point for Jules Verne. Our first guest comes from that story.

NARRATOR ONE: Our guests today are two fictional characters that Jules Verne created. I'd like to introduce our first guest.

Ladies and Gentlemen, it is my privilege to introduce Dr. Ferguson, captain of a balloon that explored Africa. Dr. Ferguson.

DR. FERGUSON: Hello. I'm Dr. Ferguson, a rich and adventurous captain of the balloon, the VICTORIA. I come from Verne's book FIVE WEEKS IN A BALLOON. This book was the first writing success of my creator. Would you like to know why the author created me?

NARRATOR ONE: Yes, please tell us, Dr. Ferguson.

DR. FERGUSON: Jules Verne and a friend built a balloon. But Verne's friend launched the balloon ahead of schedule and without Jules. Even worse, the balloon was too heavy and it crashed.

NARRATOR TWO: That's too bad. Was he angry and disappointed?

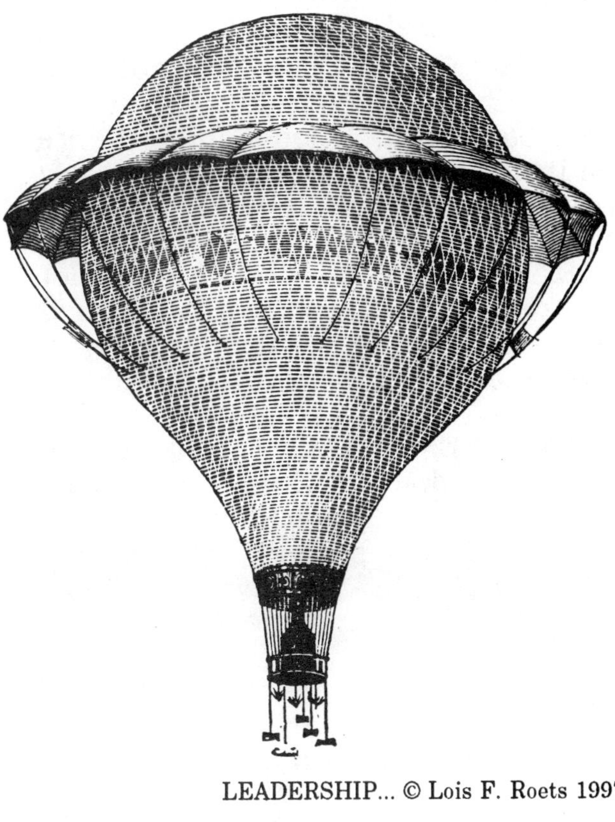

DR. FERGUSON: Certainly. He felt just like you would if a friend betrayed you. He was disappointed-just like you would be if a kite, model airplane or rocket did not fly right.

NARRATOR ONE: What did he do about the balloon failure?

DR. FERGUSON:
To make up for his disappointment, Jules escaped into the dream world of exploring in balloons. He created me, Dr.Ferguson, captain of his exploring balloon called the VICTORIA.

Our balloon was perfect. It was equipped with food, comforts, scientific equipment, and even a device for creating a new gas supply to fill the balloon.

NARRATOR TWO: What was it like - sailing above the treetops and seeing the world with the eyes of a bird?

DR. FERGUSON: Oh, it was grand! We sailed over Africa. We floated above the jungles, rivers, waterfalls, volcanoes and villages, One time our balloon's long trail rope accidentally became entangled in the tusks of a crazed wild elephant. We survived because of my great skill as a captain.

NARRATOR ONE: Don't stop now. Tell us more.

DR. FERGUSON: I can stay no longer. I must leave and return to Africa. The jungles are calling to me. *(pause and look at audience)*

Come follow me, if you dare. We travel by balloon. My crew is the most able of all balloonists. *(raises finger as if to test the wind)*.

I feel the winds. They are calling me. My crew and I must answer their call. Farewell.

NARRATOR TWO: Farewell and thank you, Dr. Ferguson. Please come to see us again. And may the winds be with you!

NARRATOR ONE: FIVE WEEKS IN A BALLOON was written in 1863. It was the first writing that brought Jules Verne to readers' attention.

Verne realized that he could take everything he had learned from his readings in science and geography, combine that knowledge with his desire for adventure, and write many stories that people liked. And if people liked reading the stories, editors would be willing to pay him for writing these stories.

NARRATOR TWO: And so Jules Verne became a recognized writer. He wrote story after story -- all combining geography, science and adventure.

His stories told about airplanes, man-made satellites, guided missiles, submarines, escalators, and television communications, many years before they were actually developed.

NARRATOR ONE: Let me introduce our other guest, Captain Nemo, designer and operator of a powerful submarine, the NAUTILUS. Captain Nemo and the Nautilus were created for the book TWENTY THOUSAND LEAGUES UNDER THE SEA.

Ladies and gentlemen, I introduce you to Captain Nemo, designer of the NAUTILUS, that fabulous undersea ship.

CAPTAIN NEMO: *(glares at audience but says nothing).*

NARRATORS ONE & TWO: *(look at each other - wondering what to do).*

NARRATOR ONE: Captain Nemo?

CAPTAIN NEMO: *(does not speak but slowly moves glaring eyes across the audience).*

NARRATOR TWO: Captain Nemo. The audience would like to know about you and your great submarine, the NAUTILUS.

CAPTAIN NEMO: Many people want to know about my ship, but I don't tell them anything. It is my ship, my submarine. I invented it. I paid workers to build it. It is mine.

NARRATOR ONE: Certainly, Captain Nemo. Certainly. We understand your desire to keep secrets of your life and of your powerful submarine. But, look at the people here today. *(Nemo look at audience).* Do they look like people who would mistreat you or steal the secrets of the submarine?

CAPTAIN NEMO: One cannot tell good or evil just by looking at people sitting near you. Good and evil are seen in the actions of each day. I trust no one.

NARRATOR TWO: Why do you not trust people? Have people harmed you? Have people harmed those you loved?

CAPTAIN NEMO: Yes. I used to be a prince in India. But the evil rulers wanted to keep all people as slaves. I could not accept slavery - for myself or for any people - particularly people who could not defend themselves.

I fought against those evil rulers of India. As punishment, the evil rulers killed my wife and two daughters.

NARRATOR TWO: That is terrible! What did you do after that happened?

CAPTAIN NEMO: I secretly took all my money and hid. I designed the NAUTILUS and hired workers to build the submarine.

Since then, my world has been below the water's surface. I come to the surface when someone needs me - someone who is good and treats all living things with respect. *(pauses).*

No further talk. I am leaving.

NARRATOR ONE: Please Captain Nemo. These people listening to you are good people. They are kind and fair to all others. Please, before you go, will you tell us some of the things that are on your submarine?

NARRATOR TWO: Please? Such knowledge would help each one of us appreciate you, the oceans, the seas, and all scientific things.

CAPTAIN NEMO: *(slowly changing his mind).* Very well. The NAUTILUS contained a large library, excellent kitchen, decompression chambers, observatory windows for watching the world below the sea. A large museum was in the NAUTILUS, as well as space for me and my crew to do our work.

NARRATOR ONE: What was it made of?

NARRATOR TWO: How was it powered?

CAPTAIN NEMO: My submarine was made of the finest steel. The entire ship was run, heated, and cooled by electrical generators I designed. We could go to great depths and yet live happily as human beings.

When we did underwater search and rescue missions, we used underwater breathing devices. You may call them aqualungs and scuba gear.

We destroyed evil people and helped those in need. (pauses)

NARRATOR ONE: Tell us more.

NARRATOR TWO: Please tell us more.

CAPTAIN NEMO: That is all I shall tell you. I must depart. I have told you what you wanted to know.

I shall now return to the cold waters of Antarctica. . *(turns to audience)*

Look out for me. If you ever try to cheat, steal, or hurt your fellow creatures, I shall find you ... and deal with you in the way I deal with all unjust persons. ... I destroy them. Beware! ... Farewell.

NARRATOR ONE: Thank you, Captain Nemo. *(nods farewell to Nemo).*

(to the audience). Captain Nemo was created for TWENTY THOUSAND LEAGUES UNDER THE SEA. He also makes a return visit in the pages of the book MYSTERIOUS ISLAND.

NARRATOR TWO: So accurately did the book TWENTY THOUSAND LEAGUES UNDER THE SEA, describe the aqualungs, decompression chambers, submarines and other devices, that 20th century scientists read Verne's book to design and improve modern submarines and other devices for underwater exploration.

In writing TWENTY THOUSAND LEAGUES UNDER THE SEA, Verne became the prophet for our future.

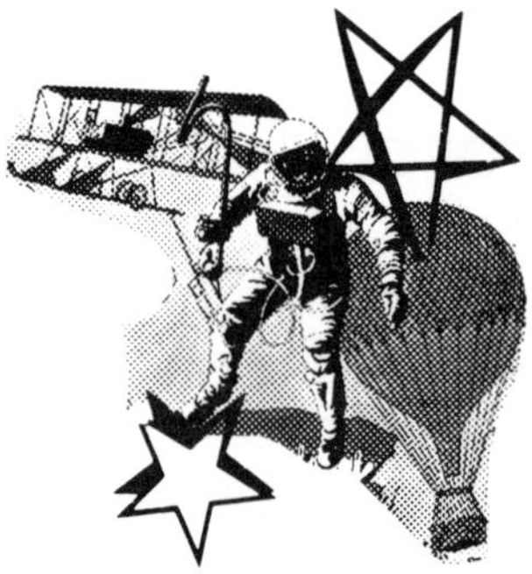

NARRATOR ONE: Jules Verne was a leader. First he led himself to read, take notes, remember and imagine. Then he led himself to write and rewrite until his stories thrilled and inspired his readers. The fictional scientific inventions of Jules Verne became blueprints for present day inventions.

One of the fictional inventions - a vehicle that combines a car, a boat and a helicopter, has not been invented. Perhaps one of *you* here today, will make that useful vehicle.

NARRATOR TWO: The old adage, *"The pen is mightier than the sword"* may or may not be true. But the pen, and the mind of the writer who uses that pen, inspires and molds the minds of people during that present generation and for many generations to come. Writers are leaders.

The End.

Leaders in Print

Category **Leaders in Print**

THIS GROUP OF PEOPLE IS IMPORTANT BECAUSE:

> *"Stories ought to judge and interpret the world."*
> *— Cynthia Ozick*

The published works of these people gave us information and ideas. They broadened our view of what life is or could be. They helped us understand our world and ourselves.

List the date of birth and death for each person listed. Describe one achievement of that person.

1. **Beatrix Potter** ______________________

2. **John Amos Comenius** ______________________

3. **Thomas Paine** ______________________

4. **Dorothea Lange** ______________________

5. **Rachel Carson** ______________________

Which writings are shaping our world today?

7 PA

Government Leaders

Some government leaders inherit their government position and some are elected by the citizens they represent. Some serve as leaders for a long time and some serve only for a short time. All government leaders possess qualities that make them effective in serving their citizens.

Directions: Match the government leader with the country served.

Canada	**England**	**France**	**Germany**	**Hawaii**
India	**Israel**	**Netherlands**	**Russia**	**United States**

Queen Beatrix ____________________

Catherine the Great ____________________

Indira Gandhi ____________________

Margaret Thatcher ____________________

Golda Meir ____________________

Pierre E. Trudeau ____________________

King Kalakaua ____________________

Frederick the Great ____________________

Charles De Gaulle ____________________

Thomas Jefferson ____________________

Directions: Read the partially completed list of qualities that help government leaders be effective. Add to that list.

1. *Ability to convince and persuade people.*
2. *Ability to know when and how to use and delegate power.*
3. *Know how to use "give and take" political maneuvering tactics.*
4. *Attract the public: Look right, talk right, appeal to value system of the majority.*
5. *Ability to determine what is important and what is not important.*
6. ____________________
7. ____________________
8. ____________________
9. ____________________
10. ____________________
11. ____________________
12. ____________________
13. ____________________
14. ____________________

Special Leaders: *Community Volunteers*

PA 8

Directions: List leaders and community services they provided.
Give each volunteer a place of honor in the **Honor Circle of Community Volunteers.**

Example: Laurie Smith - hospital volunteer, organizes summer theater workshops.

If possible, interview one of these people. *"Why do you volunteer services to this community?"*

I could volunteer my services to my community by ______________________________

____

____

9 PA

Category **People of Strong Conviction**

> *"History is a relentless master. It has no present, only the past rushing into the future. To try to hold fast is to be swept aside."*
> *— John F. Kennedy*

THIS GROUP OF PEOPLE IS IMPORTANT BECAUSE:

As a group, this group of people is often misunderstood, loved or hated — depending upon individual viewpoints. These people seemed to be driven by something within them to take a stand for their beliefs. These people did not all believe the same thing. They all, personally, did use much energy and time to promote their ideas.

* * * * * * * * * * * * * *

List the date of birth and death for each person listed. Describe one achievement for that person.

1. Clara Barton ____________________

2. Jane Addams ____________________

3. Harriet Tubman ____________________

4. Carry Amelia Nation ____________________

5. Martin Luther King, Jr. ____________________

Watch television news. Read current magazines and newspapers. Who are the "people of strong conviction" shaping our world today?

Directions:
Cut & paste a picture from the newspaper of Leader for Our Times. Complete the information. Compare your choice with choices made by others in the group.

10 PA

Leader for Our Times

Newspaper Clipping

Name of Leader: ____________________________

Leadership goal achieved: ____________________________

____

Obstacles that stood in the way of the goal:

____

____

Method(s) used to achieve the goal:

____

____

____

11 PA

Directions: Use this list and other sources of information to learn about leaders and their area of leadership.

Emmett Kelly - clown
Rudolph Nureyev - ballet
Amelia Earhart - aviation
Sequoya - Cherokee alphabet
Robert Frost - poetry
Harvey S. Firestone - tires
Johann Sebastian Bach - music
Aristotle - philosophy
Edmund Hillary - mountain climbing
Maria Montesorri - education
Harry Houdini - magic
Maria Callas - opera
George Balanchine - dance
Frank Lloyd Wright - architecture
Noah Webster - lexicography
Annie Cannon - astronomy
Helen Keller - education
Grandma Moses - art
Leta Hollingsworth - education
Valentina Tereshkova - space travel
Omar Nelson Bradley - military
Pierre Berton - television
Robert E. Lee - military
Clarence Darrow - criminal law
Robert King Merton - sociology
William Shakespeare - theater
Albert Schweitzer - medicine
Edmund Halley - comets
Wilhelm Konrad Roentgen - X-rays
Cecil Rhodes - diamonds
Annie Oakley - sharpshooting

Sigmund Freud - psychology
Phineas T. Barnum - circus
Louis Braille - writing for the blind
Amelia Bloomer - clothing fashions
August Vollmer - criminology
Sir Robert Baden-Powell - Boy Scouts
Gerhardus Mercator - mapmaking
Sophocles - plays
Louis Armstrong - musical jazz
Charles Darwin - biology
Nellie Bly - journalism
Claude Monet - art
Edward R. Murrow - news reporting
Stephen Foster - songwriting
Konrad Lorenz - ethology
Billie Jean King - tennis
Heinrich Schliemann - archeology
Dorothy Day - journalism
Louis Terman - intelligence testing
Fran Tarkenton - football
Mathew Brady - photography
Clara Barton - Red Cross
Joshua Lederberg - genetics
Ding Darling - editorial cartoons
Martin Luther - religion
Ignaz Semmelweis - medicine
Adam Smith - economics
Jascha Heifetz - violin
Auguste Rodin - sculpture
Sir Isaac Newton - gravity
John Newbery - children's books

"Speaking without thinking is shooting without aiming."

— W. G. Benham

* * * * * * * * * * * * * *

"For if the trumpet gives an uncertain sound, who shall prepare himself for battle?"

— 1 Corinthians 14:8 (BIBLE)

Language & Leadership

Language and leadership are closely related. Language is communication with others. Communications are important in planning and leading projects. Communications are important in all interpersonal relations.

We will study many different types of language. We will study: reading facial expressions, using social phrases, considering behavioral options, using and reading body language, speaking in public and other language skills.

* * * * * * * * * * * * * *

"I desire to so conduct the affairs of this administration that if, at the end, when I come to lay down the reins of power, I have lost every other friend on earth, I shall at least have one friend left, and that friend shall be down inside me."

— Abraham Lincoln

Reading Facial Expressions

A leader must know how to read faces.

Directions:
For each picture, answer these questions:

√ *Would you speak to the person?*

If **YES**, *what would you say?*

If **NO**, *why won't you speak?*

1

2

3

4

5

6

7

A leader must be able to understand the viewpoints of many people.

Different Points of View

Directions: Read each situation. Follow the directions for each.

1. **The snow is falling, light, lovely, and deep.**

What would you think about this if you were:
- a snowflake falling to the ground?
- a small child, 5 years old?
- a salesperson for snow shovels?
- a person driving to work?

2. **Vacation for the summer will soon be over.**

What would you think about this if you were:
- a student going back to school?
- a mother who daily goes to work outside the home?
- teachers in school?
- a mother in the home?
- park attendants?

3. **A wrist watch is not keeping good time.**

How would you feel about this if you were:
- the person who owned the watch?
- salesperson who sells watches?
- a watch repair person?

4. **The sun is hot, very hot. It will be very hot all day.**

What difference would this make to:
- the man who sells ice cream?
- policeman walking the streets?
- a very small baby?
- lifeguard at the swimming pool?
- mail carrier?
- an elderly person?

5. **Bobby cannot count to 100. He is in the second grade.**

What would you think about this if you were:
- Bobby?
- Bobby's friend?
- Bobby's teacher?
- Bobby's parents?
- Bobby's little sister?

6. **A holiday is approaching. You and your family are going on a trip. You suddenly get sick. You cannot go on the trip. The family decides that the trip must be cancelled for everyone.**

How would you feel about this if you were:
- the one who is sick?
- the pet dog?
- the doctor?
- another member of the family?
- travel agent?

Challenge: You write the situation. List different points of view.

____

____

____

____

____

____

____

 LL 3

Considering Behavioral Choices - Listing Possible Actions

A leader must be able to think of many ways to respond - new words or actions.

Directions: Read each situation. Answer with at least 3 suggestions for actions.

Situation One

Sam and Jason are sitting in school. Sam is tapping his pencil and pushing Jason's chair with his foot. Jason doesn't like this. He wants Sam to stop tapping the pencil and pushing the chair. What three things could Jason do?

1. ______________________________
2. ______________________________
3. ______________________________

Situation Two

You and your mother or dad have quarreled. You got angry. You said things you wish you hadn't said. What could you do now? List three possible actions.

1. ______________________________
2. ______________________________
3. ______________________________

Situation Three

You and your classmates are eating lunch. One person says something mean and untrue about another. What three things could you do?

1. ______________________________
2. ______________________________
3. ______________________________

Situation Four

You are studying. The material is difficult to learn. A test is tomorrow. What should you do today?

1. ______________________________
2. ______________________________
3. ______________________________

Situation Five

You are taking care of someone's children. They are difficult to manage. What can you do?

1. ______________________________
2. ______________________________
3. ______________________________

Using Social Expressions

A leader must know when to use, how to use, and how to accept social expressions.

Directions: *1. Use graphics and words to identify social expressions.*
(include: Please, Thank You, Compliments, Apology, Sympathetic Expressions, Encouraging / Discouraging Conversation, + others)
2. Discuss how to use and how to respond to social expressions.

Social Expressions

Using Symbols

SYMBOLS send messages without using words.

Lost and Found

Stairs Down

Directions: Draw a symbol to show each of the following:

Dangerous Dog Lives Here	**Picnic Tables**
Newspapers Sold Here	**Parking for Cars and Bicycles**
Restaurant	**Ice Cream Shop**
Quiet — Please	**Burning Leaves Not Allowed**

28

WRITTEN COMMUNICATIONS

Group sharing sessions:
What do you consider to be most important parts of *Notes & Memoes?*

What do you consider to be the most important points made in a business letter?

SOME WRITING TECHNIQUES

1. Write a rough draft first. *Read it back—outloud or into a tape recorder.*

2. Keep paragraphs short. *People tend to scan letters to see where the "meat and heart" of the letter is.*

3. State information in the positive. *Research has shown that information stated in the positive is easier to understand than sentences stated in negation.*
   Examples: Negation—difficult to understand: "This is not to say I agree with you."
   Positive—easier to understand: "I disagree with you."

4. Keep carbon copies of important letters. (Photocopy is equally suitable.)

5. When sending a message, give information on the nature of the conference, meeting etc. *A simple "See Me" causes much anxiety. The person wonders: Which one of my many transgressions has been discovered? The soap operas are filled with statements meant to cause anxiety "I need to see you." If you wish to create anxiety, tell nothing of the nature of the conference or meeting. If you wish to reduce anxiety, give more information, such as "See me—Career Education Day plans," "See me—washing the car," etc.*

6. Vary the length of the sentences. *Again, research shows us that this makes reading material easier to read.*

7. Pay attention to the layout or spacing of a page. *Could you read this page if there were no margins or all this information was in one style of print and the print was all squeezed together? Following suggestion No. 6, do you think this previous sentence is too long? What happens when you read long sentences?*

8. WRITTEN WORDS HAVE ONLY ONE CHANCE TO COMMUNICATE. Unlike speech which can be repeated and rephrased, the written word stands. And if that written word is well-stated, the written word will stand and live long. It will live in the memory of the reader—to be reread and savored.

People live through the words they write.

The Do's and Don'ts of Public Speaking

Directions: Read and study these suggestions for good public speaking.

A leader often speaks in public. To be effective, a speaker should:

DO

1. Have respect for others.
2. Listen to the other speakers so you know what is being said.
3. Be certain you have a point to make — not just a group of words.
4. Know what you want to say.
5. Express only one point or idea at a time.
6. Practice your speech aloud. If this cannot be done, mentally speak the words to make certain you know what you are going to say.
7. Take a deep breath before you begin. This supplies oxygen to your body.
8. Speak the words and ideas clearly.
9. Use proper English.
10. Realize that your voice must sound convinced. If you aren't convinced, how can you convince others? Fake calmness — if necessary.
11. Maintain composure while speaking.
12. Use proper emphasis of words and pauses when speaking.
13. Use as few words as possible.
14. Realize that every word is important — right to the end.

There are certain things an effective speaker should NOT do:

DON'T

1. Do not cut in on other speakers.
2. Do not use distracting body mannerisms — cleaning or adjusting glasses, swaying back and forth, rolling eyes, tugging at belt or collar, picking nose, twisting hair, shaking or shuffling feet and so on. These mannerisms reveal your anxiety and make you less effective. An anxious speaker is easier to defeat. Anxious speakers appear more vulnerable. Fake calmness. You can "fall apart" in private.
3. Do not use distracting speech patterns — such as repeating phrases and sounds. Examples: "Oh-h-h-h", "you know", "like I say".
4. Do not use vulgar or crude expressions. You "lose" a certain number of your listeners.
5. Do not shout or be overly dramatic except in very rare cases. All actions or movements must look as if the speaker is in control of self and the situation.
6. Do not slur, or be indistinct, on the last words. Keep clear speech to the very last word.
7. Do not mumble or repeat yourself. There is a tendency to do this at the end of a speech or statement.
8. Do not apologize for making your point. You have a right to your viewpoint and it may be expressed — once.
9. Do not monopolize (take over) the presentation.

✪ CHALLENGE: Demonstrate one or more of the "do's" or "don'ts" of public speaking.

Analyzing A Speech

LL 8

Directions: Listen to a speech (live, audiotape, radio) or watch a speech (live, videotape, documentary). Analyze it.

1. Speaker: ______________________________ Date: ________________

2. Purpose of the Speech: ____

3. Audience for whom the speech was intended:

____

4. Analysis:

Points/information presented in speech:	Appeal made to listeners: (ideals, self-worth, money....)	Techniques used: (gestures, tone ....)

LL 9

LANGUAGE AND LEADERSHIP

Preparing a Speech

SAMPLE SPEECH

TOPIC:	I LIKE BEING IN SIXTH GRADE
OPENING STATEMENT:	I like being in sixth grade. Here are some of my reasons.
SUPPORTING STATEMENTS:	As a sixth grader, I am old enough to be allowed to do many things. And yet my parents and teachers make many decisions for me. I'm glad of that. I'm not ready to make all decisions for myself. The best part of being in sixth grade is that I can do many interesting things. I can read, write and discuss points of view. When I was younger, these three things were harder for me to do.
CONCLUSION:	I suppose I'll like the 7th grade but for now, I'm quite happy to be in grade six.

SAMPLE SPEECH

The speech above shows that is has a **topic, opening statement, supporting statements** and **conclusion.**

Directions: Select a **topic.** Prepare a speech that has an **opening statement, supporting statements** and a **conclusion.** You may select a topic from those listed or you may select a topic of your own.

Physical Exercise Keeps Me Healthy
Magazines are Sources of Information
I Like Art
What I'd Do with a Million Dollars
Household Jobs I Don't Mind Doing
Household Jobs I Do Not Like To Do.
I'd Like To Change the World in These Ways
Ways I can Make the World Happier
My Favorite Forms of Exercise
Why I Like Some People More than Others
Why Some Books are More Interesting than Other Books

Speaker's choice of topic:

____

Challenge: You are a judge for a Public Speaking contest. Design a rating card for judging the speeches. Include such items as: good opening statement, clear speech, etc.

Planning Sheet for Organizing a Written or Oral Presentation

Directions: Use this form to help you prepare a speech.

TOPIC

____

OPENING STATEMENT

____

____

SUPPORT STATEMENTS

____

____

____

____

____

____

____

____

____

____

____

____

____

____

____

____

CONCLUSION

____

____

____

____

Body Language

Understanding and Using Body Language

LANGUAGE is sending and receiving messages.

BODY LANGUAGE is using the body to send or receive messages.

Directions: Read these sentences. Select a partner. One of you choose a sentence and act it out. The other must guess which sentence you are "saying" by your body language.

1. "I don't want to hear anymore about it."
2. "Yippee! I won the race."
3. "I have something in my eye and it is hurting."
4. "It's here somewhere. I know I put it in this room."
5. "Case closed. We will not discuss it."
6. "Don't bother me."
7. "Look!"
8. "Oh, you did something. I am going to tell."
9. "She combs her hair this way."
10. "You're a good doggie."
11. "I'm trying to catch a butterfly."
12. "Following a tennis match makes my eyes tired."
13. "I can hardly see it. It is so far up in the sky."
14. "That music is too loud. I can't concentrate."
15. "Pardon me? I can't hear what you are saying."
16. "I'm angry."
17. "Oh-h-h-h, my stomach hurts."
18. "Hand it to me. And I mean NOW!"
19. "You bore me."
20. "You come any closer to me and you'll get it."
21. "Ah-h-h, I get the idea now."

CHALLENGES

How do we show that we are interested in the person speaking?

____

____

____

How do we show that we are not interested in what is being said?

____

____

____

Tone of Voice; Statements of Persuasion

Communications depend upon many things: **words, facial expressions** and **body language.**

Another important part of spoken communications, is TONE OF VOICE.

Sometimes the actual words we speak are not as important as the tone of voice we use. This exercise calls your attention to the different tones of voice. It is important to use the right tone of voice with the right words.

1 *Say these words* **"I don't want any."** *Each person in the group should say this sentence using the tones of voice listed:*

casual, demanding, politely, whining, pleading, disgusted, firmly, silly

What other words can you use to describe tones of voice? Demonstrate each.

____

____

2 *Pretend you are at a meeting. Say each of these statements given below. They are often used in meetings. Each person should practice saying these sentences outloud.*

1. I don't understand that last statement. Please explain it again.
2. I object. Your statement implies that all young people are irresponsible. That simply is not the case.
3. Congratulations. That was a fine speech.
4. Elect me and I'll work to make life better for you.
5. The idea sounds good but how much time and money will it take?
6. I wish to make no comment at this time.
7. What this town needs is energetic people — people with ideas.

3 *You are still at the meeting. Select one of the topics from below and make two or three statements of persuasion about the topic. You may be agreeing with the statement or you may be disagreeing with the statement. Start your statements with the phrase "I want to speak in favor of No. 7" or "I want to disagree with statement No. 7". Then make your statements of persuasion.*

1. Everyone should vote.
2. Candy is good for everybody
3. Professional sports will, someday, ruin this country.
4. All politicians are crooks.
5. Honesty is the best policy.
6. Aggressive people always get their way.
7. Earth homes will be the homes of the future.
8. "We all learn by experience but some of us have to go to summer school." P. DeVries
9. All students should do homework every night.
10. Blaming someone for one's personal laziness is a form of lying.
11. All cooks enjoy cooking meals every day.

PUBLIC READING AS PART OF PUBLIC SPEAKING

INFORMATION

A leader must often read in public. All of the same techniques for good speaking are present in public reading. But, in this case, the words may be read rather than spoken from memory.

The only way to improve the ability to read in public is to read in public. Here are some suggestions for providing this practice.

1. Select plays and read the parts pretending you are on radio. Only the voices and sounds will be heard.

2. Select a passage from a story that has dialogue — conversation between two people. Read the selection making your voice sound like the two people.

3. Take an encyclopedia and select a paragraph that describes a person, place or thing. Read it to the group.

4. From the newspaper, select a human interest story (one about people being kind, courteous, etc.) and read it to the class.

5. Look in books of quotations, in speeches, and biography books for quotations that interest you. Read these to the group. Be certain to tell who made the statement you are quoting.

6. Study the rules of parliamentary procedure. Pretend you are the class president and you are presiding at the meeting. Follow the rules of parliamentary procedure and hold a class meeting to discuss the routine affairs, the results of last week's poster contest, and looking forward to the activities of next month. Then adjourn the meeting.

7. Prepare a newscast by taking a newspaper, cutting out the title and opening paragraph of 3 to 5 news articles. Present them as the news for the day.

8. Plan a public reading project of your own choosing.

"When Pack meets with Pack in the Jungle and
neither will go from the trail.
Lie down till the leaders have spoken —
may be fair words shall prevail."

— Rudyard Kipling

Project Planning

PROJECT PLANNING is an important part of leadership.

It is the skill of taking a complete task and breaking it into parts, assigning each part to be done and then bringing it all together again as a completed goal.

flow charts

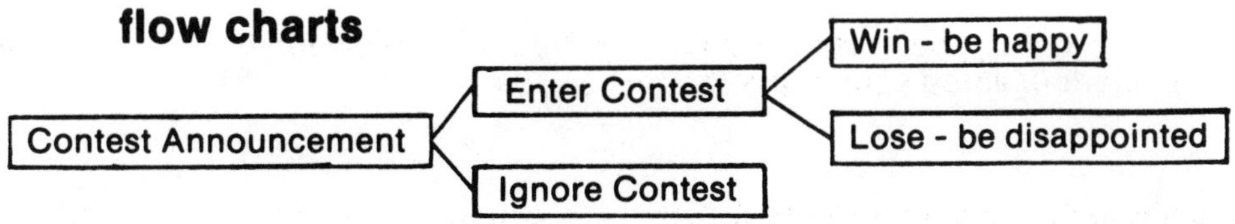

Assign Persons to Tasks at which They are Most-likely to Succees

Successful project planning often demands assigning people to do certain jobs. Some people are more suited to one job than are other people. People should be assigned jobs they can realistically do.

Directions: As a group activity, discuss, demonstrate or roleplay persons described as:

Absent-minded Albert/Alberta
Blustering Barbara/Bob
Boisterous Bill/Beebee
Calm Caleb/Corrine
Crabby Curtis/Christy
Changeable Charlie/Cheryl
Domineering Dan/Dara
Dreary Dennis/Dena
Energetic Earl/Ethel
Elegant Ethan/Ethel
Farsighted Fred/Freda
Glad Glen/Glenna
Decisive Daniel/Danielle
Harping Herman/Hanna
Impulsive Irwin/Irene
Mischievous Merle/Mildred

Neat Ned/Nora
Observing Otis/Orpha
Outspoken Omar/Odette
Powerful Paul/Pauline
Quiet Quentin/Quentina
Realistic Rayford/Rhene
Resourceful Randy/Rhonda
Sulky Sam/Susan
Silly Steve/Sally
Shrewd Sam/Sharon
Thick-headed Tom/Tonya
Tight-lipped Tony/Tina
Understanding Ulysses/Ursula
Verbal Vincent/Vernese
Willing Wilbur/Winnie

★ **CHALLENGE:** Go back over the list. Imagine a project and assign a job to 10 or 15 of the persons listed. Examples: "Quiet Quentina" may be a perfect ticket seller. She will not be tempted to spend time talking with incoming people. "Energetic Earl" will do well on the cleanup committee for a party. "Sulky Susan" should be in charge of one detail where she works alone. She will not work well with others.

Projects: Listing Supplies

Directions: *Read the project title listed in each box. Below each title is a list. Circle those items necessary to complete the project listed. Cross out those items not needed for the project. List other items - if other items are needed.*

Polish Shoes	Other Items	Wash the Dishes	Other Items
shoe shine brush or cloth		curtains for window	
flowers	____________	soap	____________
magazine	____________	water	____________
pair of shoes	____________	dirty dishes	____________
window	____________	towels for drying	____________

Wrap a Gift	Other Items	Paint a Picture	Other Items
a gift		brushes	
box of nails	____________	paint	____________
wrapping ribbon	____________	large umbrella	____________
tape	____________	canvas or paper	____________
pen	____________	slippers	____________

Birthday Party	Other Items	Cleaning Your Room	Other Items
guest list		broom	
games	____________	candle	____________
Christmas tree	____________	dustpan	____________
prizes	____________	box of candy	____________
lunch	____________	box for toys	____________
balloons	____________	wastepaper bin	____________

Cut and Rake the Lawn	Other Items	Setting the Table	Other Items
rake		mirror	
stones	____________	dishes	____________
lawn mower	____________	silverware	____________
ring on your finger	____________	rugs	____________
glass of lemonade	____________	glasses	____________
gloves	____________	table	____________

Listing Materials To Complete A Project

Directions: For each project named, list the materials and supplies you would need to complete that project. *If needed, give the cost of each item.*

1. FAMILY PICNIC IN THE BACK YARD

2. RACES AT THE PARK FOR AGES 8-12

3. PUTTING ON A PLAY FOR A READING GROUP

4. BABYSITTING FOR TWO PRESCHOOL CHILDREN

5. WASHING A CAR

6. WRITING A REPORT

7. STARTING A LAWNCUTTING BUSINESS

8. PLANNING A SCIENTIFIC EXPERIMENT

Project Planning: Raising Fresh Vegetables

Leaders are able to plan projects.
A successful project plan requires:
1. Knowledge of materials needed to complete the project.
2. Cost estimate of the materials - if cost is a consideration.
3. Awareness of the first step that should be taken.

Directions: List the materials needed for the project named on this page. If needed, give the cost of each item. Circle the first item that will be used.

Project: ______________________________

Materials Add more information - if you wish. **Cost**

Flowchart for Project Planning — Sequence of Events

This type of flowchart is suitable for planning a sequence of events, listing person in charge of that event and listing task description.

PROJECT GOAL

SEQUENCE OF EVENTS

PERSON IN CHARGE

TASK DESCRIPTION

Additional Notes:

Flowchart for Project Planning — Sequence of Events

This type of flowchart is suitable for planning a sequence of events, listing person in charge of that event and listing task description.

COMPLETED SAMPLE

PROJECT GOAL

Hobby Fair

SEQUENCE OF EVENTS	PERSON IN CHARGE	TASK DESCRIPTION
Chair Program Get all permissions	Bob and Sally	get things started
Establish committees	Bob and Sally	appoint a chair for each committee
Establish rules for entries - Assign to committee	Committee chair: Jean	be specific what may NOT be entered
Publicity: students, teachers parents, press	Committee Chair: Jason	be sure notice to parents is very clear that school doesn't accept responsibility for breakage
Prepare exhibit hall	Committee Chair: Peter	get display tables - plan schedule for supervising exhibits
Judging: get judge, design judging form	Committee chair: Amy	print extra judging forms
Awards: who should get them, and what they will be	Committee chair: Meri	$50.00 limit

Additional Notes: Coordinator for all is the teacher. All major decisions must be cleared with teacher. Remember: each entrant thinks their own entry is the most important. Try to be as attentive to each entrant as possible.

Flowchart Planning A Project — Committees Required

List the overall goal , each committee and then fill in what are the **specific jobs of that committee.**

Overall Goal

COMMITTEE

COMMITTEE

COMMITTEE

COMMITTEE

Additional Notes:

Flowchart Planning A Project — Committees Required

List the overall goal each committee and then fill in what are the **specific jobs of that committee.**

COMPLETED SAMPLE

Overall Goal

Class Party For Grade 5

COMMITTEE
Entertainment
Chairperson: Mary

Games - Bob and Mary

Prizes - Tim and Jill

COMMITTEE
Food—Lunch
Chairperson: Scott

Sandwiches - Jack and Tom

Cake - Betty

Orange juice - Amy and Ann

Napkins, etc. - Scott

COMMITTEE
Decorations
Chairperson: Russell

Ribbons - Charlotte

Signs - Russell

COMMITTEE
Clean-Up
Chairperson: Oscar

Sweep floors - Peggy

Wash desktops - Ron

Remove decorations - Charlotte and Russell

Additional Notes: All student plans must be approved by teacher. Total cost of prizes may not exceed $5.00. If someone cannot do the assigned work, that person is responsible for getting a substitute. All substitutes must be reported to the committee chairperson.

Group Dynamics: Problems

There are times when an individual works alone.
There are other times when individuals must work together.
Working as a group is called group dynamics.

Twist an arm -
forcing the issue or opinion

Segregate one from
the rest of the group.

Make fun of another.

Prevent another from speaking.

Directions: Here are some examples of problems that can happen in group dynamics. Add your own ideas.

46

PP 8

Group Dynamics: Consensus-Building

There are times when an individual works alone.
There are other times when individuals must work together.
Working as a group is called group dynamics.

Working together
for a common goal!

Directions: Write or draw your ideas of how individuals within a group can work to build group consensus.

Understanding Your Abilities and Desires in Project Participation

In all situations, you must select to do one of three behaviors:

LEAD **FOLLOW** **GET OUT OF THE WAY**

BRAINSTORM: How do you know if you should LEAD, FOLLOW or GET OUT OF THE WAY? Be sure to include such items as knowledge, ability to convince people, sufficient time and similar considerations.

Directions: Read each goal. Decide if you would like to LEAD, FOLLOW or GET OUT OF THE WAY. Notice that all people do not like to lead in the same situations. This is necessary for society to function smoothly.

GOAL ONE: Clean the house. One other person will help you.

GOAL TWO: Plan a Hobby Sharing Fair for grades kindergarten - grade six.

GOAL THREE: Plan a program that will make it possible for you and three friends to earn money on Saturday afternoon.

GOAL FOUR: Organize a ping pong tournament.

GOAL FIVE: Organize students of your class into groups for writing a classroom newspaper.

GOAL SIX: Plan a garden on a plot of ground 6 feet x 6 feet.

GOAL SEVEN: Organize a fund-raising bake sale.

GOAL EIGHT: Plan a one-half hour holiday program for your class.

GOAL NINE: Plan a one-half hour party for your classroom.

GOAL TEN: Write a plan for painting the outside of the garage.

GOAL ELEVEN: Organize a baby-sitting clinic. This is a training session for young people to learn how to take care of children.

GOAL TWELVE: Write a plan that would make a perfect day at school.

Share your decisions to LEAD, FOLLOW or GET OUT OF THE WAY with the others in your group.

CHALLENGE: List two or more plans that you'd like to LEAD; two or more - FOLLOW; and two or more - GET OUT OF THE WAY.

LEAD ______________________________

____

____

FOLLOW ______________________________

____

____

GET OUT OF THE WAY ______________________________

____

____

Should I:
Lead? Follow? Get out of the way?

10
PP

The most important part of leadership is sincere respect for the actions and decisions of others. Each of us has a right to make decisions. This right must be accepted and respected.

This worksheet will help you decide if you should **lead** *(be in charge)*, **follow** *(be supportive of the one in charge)*, or **get out of the way.**

1. List the goal or purpose of the project (be specific): ______________________________

____

2. Fill in this information:

Supplies	**Persons with whom I would work**
Brief plan of action	

3. Answer these questions:

1. I believe in the goal. _____Yes _____No _____I don't know
2. I have time to give to this project. _____Yes _____No _____Doubtful
3. I have sufficient physical energy for this project. _____Yes _____No _____Doubtful
4. I have sufficient mental reserves to manage this project. _____Yes _____No _____Doubtful
5. I have a brief plan that I think will work. _____Yes _____No _____Doubtful
6. I believe I could guide or lead the persons involved. _____Yes _____No _____Doubtful

4. CONSIDERATIONS

1. If you answered YES to No. 1 and YES to two or more of items Numbers 2 - 6, consider being the leader for the project.
2. If you answered YES to No. 1 and NO to three or more of Numbers 2 - 6, consider being the follower or supporter of the leader.
3. If you answered NO to No. 1, choose one of two actions:
   Choice A: Do not get involved in any way (praise, criticism)
   Choice B: Lead the opposition to oppose the goal or redirect it.

11 PP

Troubleshooting

A "troubleshooter" identifies the problem and finds ways to get rid of the problem. A leader is a troubleshooter.

*Directions: For each project shown, list the **task**, the **problem**, and at least two **solutions**.*

Task: A lady must shop for many items.

Problem: She has many heavy packages to carry.

Solutions: ____________________

____

____

Task: ____________________

Problem: ____________________

Solutions: ____________________

____

____

Task: ____________________

Problem: ____________________

Solutions: ____________________

____

____

Debate & Discussion

THE ABILITY TO DEBATE AND DISCUSS ISSUES IS VITAL TO SUCCESSFUL LEADERSHIP. IT IS THROUGH DEBATE AND DISCUSSION THAT IDEAS TAKE SHAPE, AND ARE TESTED WITH OTHER INTERESTED PEOPLE. LEADERS MUST ALWAYS BE AWARE OF WHAT OTHERS ARE THINKING AND FEELING.

Definitions

debate: to state arguments for or against a particular issue.

discussion: a verbal interchange of two or more persons expressing ideas about a particular topic or issue.

To debate and discuss, you need:

1. knowledge about the issue
2. insight to determine which information is of major importance and which information is of minor importance.
3. decision-making ability based on information learned through the exchange of ideas

GROUP SHARING OF IDEAS AND TECHNIQUES

1. What is a leader?

2. What kinds of people make good leaders?

3. What kinds of decisions are hardest for you?

4. Do you prefer to lead yourself or lead others?

5. Do you prefer to compete with yourself or compete with others?

6. What ways to you have of making yourself consider other actions—rather than do the first action that comes to your mind?

7. Have you been the leader for a project? How did it feel to be the leader?

8. If you could solve one problem—what would that problem be?

Understanding Listening and Restatement of an Idea

BRAINSTORM:

1. Why are listening skills important?
2. What are good listening skills?
3. Why must an effective leader be a good listener?

> RESTATING THE ISSUE OR IDEA
> In problem solving, arguments, discussion and general conversation, it is sometimes advisable to restate what was just said. This helps to clarify the issue and to consider it a second time.

Directions: Work with a partner or very small group. One person reads one of these statements. The other restates the issue or idea by rephrasing. Be careful not to change the meaning of the statement.

1. I don't care what you get me for my birthday as long as it is big and expensive.
2. I don't like school except for reading, math, spelling and social studies.
3. The problem today is that most people think money can buy answers to problems but that is one thing money usually cannot do.
4. Music, art and the human spirit speak a universal language.
5. People who wear jewelry wear it because they wish to look and feel more lovely to self and others.
6. Eating in a restaurant by candlelight is fine but, with such dim light, how can I tell if there is a fly in my soup?
7. After reading political speeches for the last forty years, I see that every year people think taxes are too high and services are too few.
8. I can't understand why I am tired this evening. All I did was to scrub and wax two floors, attend to two loads of laundry, take care of three preschool kids and run a few errands.
9. He is very persuasive. He could sell an electric heater to a person living at the equator and make that person think the heater would serve a good purpose.
10. It is not possible to learn new viewpoints if you continuously talk to the same people.
11. Dominoes, checkers and card games are enjoyed by all ages because there are different levels of skills that can be mastered.
12. Sometimes I buy breakfast cereal, not because I know I like it, but because the advertising makes me think I will like it.
13. I'd like to be a great athlete but I really don't like to do exercises, follow certain eating and sleeping habits, keep in training or take part in competition.
14. Rollerskating is unsafe for everyone. I should know because I once broke my leg while rollerskating.
15. After seeing holes in the soles and splits in the seams, it is safe to say that these shoes are wearing out.
16. The teacher picks on me — just because I didn't have my homework done for 3 days.

✪ CHALLENGE: Select any topic, speak to the topic, and then present the same idea in different words.

PARAPHRASING

DIRECTIONS: Use your own words to paraphrase or restate these common expressions, cliches and idioms.

Don't count your chickens until they are hatched.
He was caught red-handed.
A bird in the hand is worth two in the bush.
This is like trying to find a needle in the haystack.
Let sleeping dogs lie.
Let's settle this and bury the hatchet.
All that glitters is not gold.
Slow and steady wins the race.
You can't tell the book by its cover.
He speaks out of both sides of his mouth.
It happened out of the blue.
It is raining cats and dogs.
They fit like two peas in a pod.
Stop this monkey business.
He was stopped cold.
Shape up or ship out.
Secure as a clam at high tide.
This is bringing coals to Newcastle.
He bought a pig in a poke.
A fool and his money are quickly parted.
He's a chip off the old block.
Better late than never.
This situation is a can of worms.
Every cloud has a silver lining.
Happiness is its own reward.
Let bygones be bygones.
The pen is mightier than the sword.
Don't build air castles in the sky.

4 DD

Island Survival

You will spend 5 days alone on a remote island. Someone will bring you there the morning of the first day and will return the evening of the 5th day. Fresh water, palm trees & firewood are on the island. Don't count on other things!

Directions:
List 20 items you will bring with you.

1. ______
2. ______
3. ______
4. ______
5. ______
6. ______
7. ______
8. ______
9. ______
10. ______
11. ______
12. ______
13. ______
14. ______
15. ______
16. ______
17. ______
18. ______
19. ______
20. ______

Cooperation? Persuasion? Coercion? Control?
Assistance? Mutual Support? Friendship?

Call it anything you wish. The fact is: There are times when a leader must have the cooperation from the others. Getting this cooperation is a challenge to a leader. A leader may get cooperation through responsible and fair means. Or, the leader may try to force cooperation by irresponsible, dishonest or dishonorable means. Every person should be aware of fair and unfair means of getting cooperation.

Directions: Listed below are techniques used to get people to do as the leader wishes. 1)Read the technique. 2) Understand the technique. 3) Answer this question: "If the project or issue is important, is the technique honest, fair, and just?"

5 DD

1. **"I am older than you so you have to do as I say."**

2. **"I have authority over you. Therefore, you must do as I say."**

3. **Divide and conquer.**
   ''Divide and conquer'' is a technique where you get part of the group to go against the other part.

4. **"Loyalty demands that you go along with me."**

5. **"If you don't do as I say, you will be sorry."**
   The leader makes you cooperate by making you afraid of personal punishment, loss of prestige, financial ruin, and other undesirable results.

6. **Feed the fires of ambition.**
   This technique convinces people that, if they cooperate and help, their own desires will be met.

7. **"Cooperate, or your life will be unbearable."**
   This is another form of creating fear, particularly the fear of the unknown.''

8. **"You have to help me because I helped you."**
   This is a bad situation when you ''owe'' somebody because of a past situation. Never accept a favor if that favor will make you ''owe'' somebody a favor.

9. **Appeal to a person's generosity and kindness.**
   Some people feel a great obligation to help others. They have a hard time saying ''no'' to a request. Some leaders use this inability to say ''no'' to force assistance.

10. **Suggest rejection by loved ones, peers, family.**
    This technique suggests that you must give cooperation. Because, if you don't, you will have disappointed your friends, family, and loved ones.

11. Undermine self-confidence to force cooperation.
This technique suggests that you aren't worth much, that your ideas don't count. If you decided to give cooperation, your help wouldn't be of much value. The technique is accomplished by: harsh ''put-down'' words and actions, overlooking a person, and belittling someone in public.

12. Buying cooperation by gifts, words or actions.
This technique is related to No. 8. People who attempt to buy cooperation often give gifts, tell personal confidences, and take the blame for another. These actions are supposed to ''buy'' the other person to be cooperative.

13. Guilt trip.
The guilt trip could also be called the guilt trap. Guilt is a sentence we pass on ourselves because we have disappointed ourselves. We have been less of a person than we could have been. We feel guilty when we hurt a person, when we have betrayed friendship, and in many other situations. Some leaders attempt to make you feel guilty if you elect to ''get out of the way.'' They attempt to make you feel that it is **your** job to make **their** project succeed. Feel guilty when it is self-imposed; not when it is other-imposed.

What other ways do people use to make you do something or support a cause?

Tolerance for Diversity

DD 6

Appreciate the diversity - the variety - that exists among friends, family members, classmates, communities and nations.

Directions: List words or actions that represent a non-tolerant attitude. On the opposite side, list words or actions that show a tolerant attitude.

Non-tolerant ☞ ☞ ☞ ☞☞ ☞ ☞ Tolerant

Example:
Why can't they be like us? ☞☞ ☞☞ *Life is interesting when people are different.*

Emotional Moments

Leaders are often confronted by those who do not agree with them. These confrontations are highly charged with emotion. The leader must think fast, and think of some way to respond to save personal dignity and respect for the leadership he or she exerts. In these three situations the leader is **B**, the confronter is **A**.

Directions:
Look at the three situations.
You are B, the leader.
How would you, the leader (B) ,
deal with the confronter (A) ?

Situation One:

Situation Two:

Situation Three:

Problem Recognition & Solution Guide

Directions: Use this Problem Recognition & Solution Guide for personal and/or group problems.

Problem Recognition:

1. Identify the situation that needs a solution:

Solution Guide:

2. Who wants a solution:

3. Who needs a solution:

4. Identify the "givens" - those factors that are known: people, cost, limitations, resources..... :

5. Identify the "not-givens" - those factors you don't know but wish you knew: attitudes, outcome of vote,.... :

6. Describe or draw the ideal solution - as you now see it:

7. My plan for implementing the solution:

9 DD

PROBLEM SOLVING

Problem solving is needed by every person every day. Some problems are easily solved. Some problems need much thought.

PROBLEM SOLVING, in its simplest form, demands:

1. Statement of the problem
2. Listing of possible solutions
3. Selecting best solution
4. Implementing the solution

WORKSHEET FOR <u>PROBLEM SOLVING</u>

1 State the problem in clear, precise terms. State one issue only.

2 List at least five (no less) possible solutions.

3 Select the solution that you think is best. State it here.

4 Develop an implementation plan to put the selected solution into practice.

Group work: review the problem, possible solutions, selected solution, implementation plan, with others. Evaluate their comments.

Spotlight on:

In the provided circle, spotlight a person, cause or event.
What is the reason for the spotlight?

62

Risk!

What does risk look like? What words describe it?

63

12 DD

Terms & Concepts of Contemporary Leadership

Directions: Give an example of each term or concept.
Add to the definition - if you wish.

Propaganda - publicity you want someone to believe.

Example:

Public Perception - what the public believes to be true.

Example:

"Spin" - the interpretation you put to an event.

Example:

Micro-manage a Situation - tendency of a leader to do everything instead of delegating some tasks to others.

Example:

Teacher Helps

(Instructor's Manual Teacher Helps. pp.91-100)

INSTRUCTIONAL MODEL FOR LEADERSHIP *

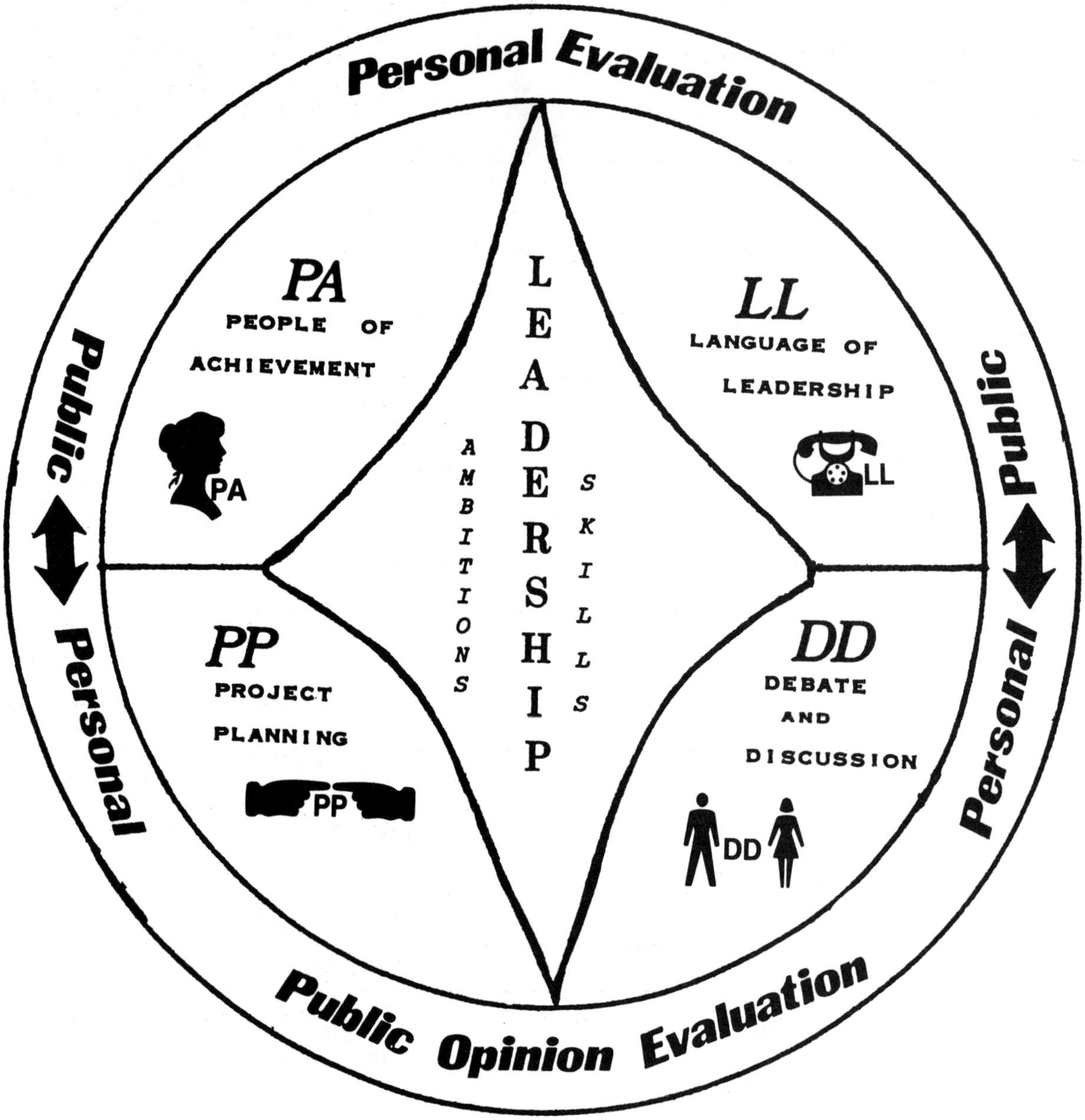

INSTRUCTIONAL MODEL FOR LEADERSHIP — SKILLS TRAINING PROGRAM

There are four major components to leadership:
PEOPLE OF ACHIEVEMENT (PA) — provides role models and fires ambition.
LANGUAGE OF LEADERSHIP (LL) — assists ambitious leader in mastering language skills such as public speaking, reading faces, etc.
PROJECT PLANNING (PP) — teaches necessary skills to break a large project into smaller workable units and then put it back together.
DEBATE AND DISCUSSION (DD) — opens mind to value of opinions of others as well as confidence to express personal opinions.

LEADERSHIP, a combination of ambitions and skills, forms the center.
EVALUATION, by self and the public through public opinion, surrounds all.

Believe in yourself to be a leader. Lead yourself, and when the time and cause are right, lead others.

Leadership Project - A Plan

Student Name ______________________________ *Plan Date* __________

1. Leadership Project (describe):

____

____

2. Leadership of ____ self and/or _____ others.

3. Actions/events to accomplish this leadership project:

____

____

____

____

____

____

____

____

____

4. The first step to accomplish this leadership project:

____

____

5. Results - judging the project:

Not a success because: ____

Somewhat successful because: __________________________________

Moderately successful because: _________________________________

Quite successful because: _____________________________________

- Project abandoned because ____________________________________

  ____.

6. Other comments:

____

____

____

Suggestions for Project Planning

1. Select a famous person and do a study of his or her life.
2. Make a set of flashcards using persons names on one side and achievements on the other side.
3. Make a collection of pictures of faces. Use these as starters for creative writing or discussion of dealing with certain situations.
4. Make a list and illustrate all the nonverbal communications you see around you.
5. Write a report on the value of signs and symbols.
6. Use body language to give a message. Someone should guess your message.
7. Use body language to interpret a piece of music.
8. Talk to someone who knows sign language. Learn the alphabet. Demonstrate the alphabet to your class.
9. Write a message in Morse code. Your friend decodes and returns the message — all in Morse Code.
10. Plan a Hobby Sharing Fair for your class.
11. Select a favorite story book. Give a description of the personality types shown in the book.
12. Interview a writer of stories. Learn how that person creates a character for a story.
13. List all projects you'd like to accomplish during your lifetime. Divide the list according: before age 18, from ages 19-30 and after 31.
14. If your school doesn't have a student council, plan one.
15. Describe the perfect society — the rules by which people can live together in peace and harmony.
16. Originate a new game. Plan it, write the rules, teach the game to others.
17. Plan an exhibit of original art work for the students in your school.
18. Plan a yearly program which will invite at least one famous civic leader, artist, writer and musician into your school.
19. You want to earn $100 in a selling project. Write a plan of action.
20. Make a collection of famous quotations that appeal to you.
21. Do research to determine the number of minutes of commercial time is present in a one hour TV program.
22. Interview at least 3 teachers and ask them what kinds of students they like to teach.
23. Plan a science fair exhibit in which all exhibits must be of moving parts but are not run by batteries.
24. Design a research project that will analyze the kinds of advertising present in a given magazine.
25. There will be a fundraising paperdrive. Plan the drive that will give the most efficient use of time and raise the most money.
26. Organize bicycle races for your school holiday.
27. Plan a poetry contest, or original song contest or story contest.
28. Plan a parents night at school.
29. Plan and complete an anti-vandalism campaign in your school.

SUGGESTED PROBLEMS FOR PROBLEM SOLVING

1. What is the best way to keep toys in good working order?
2. In what way could I keep my garden free from weeds?
3. What is the best plan to reduce accidents on the playground?
4. What is the best way to reduce vandalism in our school?
5. How can we design an energy efficient home?
6. In what ways could we reduce inflation?
7. In what ways could students earn money doing odd jobs in the neighborhood?
8. How could a student make better use of study time?
9. What kinds of new transportation are needed in this country?
10. How could we improve the efficiency of the summer clean-up crew that works in the school during the summer?
11. How might we reduce waste of food at hot lunch school programs?
12. What kinds of contests could be sponsored that would encourage people to do more reading?
13. How could we reduce hunger in all countries?
14. In what ways can we reward polite behavior?
15. In what ways could we make our school buses more safe for the riders?
16. In what ways could students improve in writing skills?
17. What is the best way to raise money for a program?
18. In what ways could we reduce taxes and still provide services?
19. In what ways could we increase good nutrition for all people?
20. In what ways could we reduce alcoholic consumption in people under age 18?
21. In what ways could we make people over 18 reduce alcoholic consumption?
22. What is our most serious problem today?
23. In what ways could the government encourage saving of earned money?
24. When you are babysitting, what is the best way to keep your charges happy?
25. What is the major problem facing travelers in space?
26. What is the best way to keep a house clean?
27. How can we decrease fear of death?
28. What can be done to encourage acceptance of different cultures and minorities?
29. In what ways could we encourage cooperation with nature (rather than dominance of nature)?
30. In what ways could we increase appreciation of poetry?
31. What is the easiest way to learn to swim?
32. What would be the biggest problem if all cash were eliminated and all bills were paid by credit cards?
33. How could we reduce interest rates?
34. In what ways could we reduce low employment rates for college graduates?

Newspaper and magazine articles suggest many other issues.

Recognizing Leadership in Students

(an informal identification/recognition procedure)

There are two theories of Leadership: **Trait Leadership** and **State Leadership**.

Trait Leadership suggests that leadership is part of one's personality. A person with Trait Leadership tends to "take over", "be in charge", initiate or assume responsibility for many tasks or causes. While not always being exercised, it is evident across a lifetime. Trait Leadership is part of the person's perception and expression of self and life.

State Leadership suggests that a person "takes over" or "assumes responsibility" for a specific cause - a specific state or condition. State Leadership empowers the person to "rise to the occasion" when energy and organization are needed to accomplish a specific goal for self or community. State Leadership may not be present across a lifetime. It is used and developed only when needed.

✍ Recommendation for Leadership Recognition or Opportunities ✍

I recommend student ________________________________ for leadership.

This recommendation is based on this observation (describe):

____

____

____

____

____

Based on the above-described observation, I recommend:

❑ recognition/award (Suggestion) ________________________________

❍ opportunities (Suggestions: classes in leadership, projects, tasks, mentorship, ... - describe, please)

____

____

Recommendation made by:
Teacher/adult ________________________________ Date ____________

❋ ❋ ❋ - - - **follow-through action(s):**

Describe follow-through action(s).
Please include: action, date, person providing follow-through procedure(s).

____

____

____

____

- -

70

RATING SCALE FOR LEADERSHIP
A Self-rating Scale by Dr. Lois Roets

Name________________________________ Age________ Grade________ Date________________

DIRECTIONS: Read each statement. Mark with the number of your choice.

1—almost always 2—quite often 3—sometimes 4—not very often 5—never

____ I have strong convictions about things.

____ When I believe in something, I work to promote it.

____ I listen to both sides of the issue before I make up my mind.

____ I have self-confidence.

____ I am able to say my opinions in public.

____ I usually am satisfied with the decisions I make.

____ When I am criticized for some action I have taken, I can usually go about my work.

____ I like to be in charge of events.

____ I am able to see what materials are needed to complete a project.

____ I am able to see the sequence of steps necessary to complete a project.

____ When I am convinced of something, I have courage to act for it.

____ I often lead in projects.

____ When I see somebody who is a leader, I think that I could do as well as that leader.

____ I can speak to persons in authority.

____ I have energy to complete projects that I am interested in completing.

____ I can understand the viewpoints of others.

____ I am willing to change my mind if new facts suggest that I should change my mind.

____ I get anxious and excited and am able to use this energy to complete a task.

____ I am able to work with many types of persons and personalities.

____ I usually understand the plot of a story or play or the main point in a conversation.

____ I am willing to try new experiences when these seem wise.

____ I know when to lead, to follow and to get out of the way.

____ I admire people who have achieved great things.

____ I dream of the day and time when I am able to lead myself or others to great accomplishment.

____ I feel at ease asking people for help or information.

____ I can be a "peacemaker" if I want to be.

Readings - Books

Directions: Read books about leaders.
List the leader's name and the area of leadership.
List: title, author, publisher, copyright date, number of pages.
Rate the book (The book was:...). Add one comment.

Leader : ______________________ Area of Achievement:________________

Book Title: ______________________________________

Author: ______________________________________

Publisher : __________________________ Copyright Date:_____ No. of pages:_____

The book was: *excellent* *average* *of little interest* *of no interest* *definitely not my type.*

Comment(s)

Leader : ______________________ Area of Achievement:________________

Book Title: ______________________________________

Author: ______________________________________

Publisher : __________________________ Copyright Date:_____ No. of pages:_____

The book was: *excellent* *average* *of little interest* *of no interest* *definitely not my type.*

Comment(s)

Leader : ______________________ Area of Achievement:________________

Book Title: ______________________________________

Author: ______________________________________

Publisher : __________________________ Copyright Date:_____ No. of pages:_____

The book was: *excellent* *average* *of little interest* *of no interest* *definitely not my type.*

Comment(s)

Readings - Magazines & Newspapers

Directions: Read magazine & newspaper articles about leaders.
List the leader's name and the area of leadership.
List: article title, author (if listed), publication name, publication date, page number.
Rate the book (The book was:...). Add one comment.

Leader : ______________________ Area of Achievement:________________

Article Title: ______________________________________

Author (if listed): ______________________________________

Publication Name : __________________________ Date:________ Page Number:_____

The article was: *excellent* *average* *of little interest* *of no interest* *definitely not my type.*

Comment(s)

Leader : ______________________ Area of Achievement:________________

Article Title: ______________________________________

Author (if listed) : ______________________________________

Publication Name : __________________________ Date:_____ Page Number:_____

The article was: *excellent* *average* *of little interest* *of no interest* *definitely not my type.*

Comment(s)

Leader : ______________________ Area of Achievement:________________

Article Title: ______________________________________

Author (if listed) : ______________________________________

Publication Name: __________________________ Date:_____ Page Number:_____

The article was: *excellent* *average* *of little interest* *of no interest* *definitely not my type.*

Comment(s)

Student Evaluation for the
LEADERSHIP TRAINING PROGRAM

1. I liked studying about people of achievement *Yes No Sometimes*

2. I learned more ways to communicate with people. *Yes No Maybe*

3. I have practiced being a better listener. *Yes No Maybe*

4. I am comfortable speaking my ideas. *Yes No I'm getting better at it*

5. I know how to plan a project. *Yes No I'm getting better at it.*

6. I can work alone or with others. *Yes No I'm getting better at it.*

7. I know when to ***Lead, Follow***, or ***Get Out of the Way***. *Yes No Sometimes*

8. I learned new ideas from others in the leadership group. *Yes No Maybe*

9. What did you like best about the Leadership Program?

____

____

10. How would you improve the Leadership Program?

____

____

Comments you'd like to make:_______________________________

____

____

____

Participant's Signature ______________________ *Date* __________

LEADERSHIP

This certificate is issued

to

____

for

full participation in

LEADERSHIP

______________ ______________

Instructor Date

EXCELLENT ACHIEVEMENT AWARD

Issued to ______________________________

For This Achievement:

____

____

____

____

Date:______________ Issued by:

Use with Badge-a-Minit™ or other badge/button maker.

Use with
Badge-a-Minit™
or other
badge/button
maker.

Notes

Instructor's Manual

How to Use the
Leadership Training Program, Ages 8-18.

Program Flexibility
There is no right or wrong way to use this program. Use all of the Leadership program, or only those parts that will meet your needs. Use the program as the author developed it. Or, use the ideas suggested here to create your own program.

Time & Length of Leadership Training Program
Determine ahead of time how much time you will have for the Leadership program. Then select some of each section: PA, LL, PP, DD, and use them with students. Do well what you elect to do, rather than do many activities superficially.

Age Suitability
This program has been used extensively for ages 8-18. Young students have completed some of the activities when they are paired with other students.

Student Participation
Students should freely choose to participate or to continue the Leadership program. Some students benefit from formal leadership programs. Others choose to exercise leadership and learn skills as they exercise leadership.

Preparation for Using the Leadership Program
Familiarize yourself with the instructional model; all of the activities - People of Achievement (PA), Language of Leadership (LL), Project Planning (PP), and Debate and Discussion (DD);and Teacher Helps. Then select the activities and sequence appropriate to the group of students participating in the Leadership Program. Use the entire program or only specific activities.

Personality qualities of a leader are:
- *Strong conviction on certain issues.*
- *Sufficient self-confidence to accept praise and blame.*
- *Courage to see through planning and implementation of a project.*
- *Sufficient physical and emotional energies required for the task.*
- *Sense of balance and proportion for the energies given and results received.*
- *Planning ability which breaks a large project into small workable units.*
- *Wise use of tension that works for self, instead of against self.*
- *Desire to be a leader.*

LEAD YOURSELF
BE A LEADER
LEAD OTHERS

(PA) People of Achievement - Instructor's Manual

Objectives:

1. Acquaint students with role models of achievers as leaders.
2. Understand that achievers are leaders who achieved in a particular area of accomplishment. Their accomplishments influenced others.
3. Become aware that certain groups of achievers share common habits and attitudes.
4. Nurture personal ambition to achieve.

> Activities in People of Achievement (PA) help students become aware of leaders and their achievements. Instructors determine which PA activities will be completed and how much time to spend on the PA section. Select the PA activities that will meet your teaching abilities and the needs of the students.

PA-People of Achievement

PA-1. Wanted: Leadership in Many Areas p.6

Leaders exert leadership to improve situations. At any point in history, more improvements need to be made. Some suggestions for improvement are given. Students should add more suggestions for improvements.

Suggestions: heated and cooled shoes & socks, small and cheaper computers, telephones that translate foreign languages, clothes that expand and contract with body size ...

PA-2. Milton Hershey: Chocolate King pp.7-9.

Use the reader's theater to introduce Hershey and his method for success. More information may be added from encyclopedia entries for Milton Hershey, the chocolate industry, and the city of Hershey, PA.

Other related topics of interest are: histories of specialty candy, toy, games, ice cream, soft drinks, and the people responsible for developing each.

PA-3. Inventors. p.10.

Bell - telephone	Birdseye - frozen foods	Colt - revolver
Edison - light	Galileo - thermometer	Gillette - razor
Gutenberg - movable type	Hunt - safety pin	Judson - zipper
Land - camera	Lippershey-telescope	McCormick - reaper
Morse - telegraph	Waterman - pen	Whitney - cotton gin

PA-4. Inventors and Inventions. p.11.

Answers will vary. Students should give reasons for choices of inventions that they think significantly changed the world.

Suggestions may include: wheel, fire, engines, medicines, plastic...

PA-5. Jules Verne. pp.12-16.

Before reading the play, display books written by Jules Verne. Keep them displayed during the leadership sessions. Students should understand the importance and foresight of Verne for underwater exploration, search, rescue.

- To help the audience to identify the readers, four signs are suggested: **Narrator One, Captain Nemo, and Dr. Ferguson, Narrator Two.** That is also the suggested arrangement of the four speakers: two narrators on the end with Nemo and Ferguson in the center.

PA-6. Leaders in Print. p.17.

Writings, photographs, and illustrations which appear in print have a great effect upon readers and viewers. Each of the five listed in PP-6 contributed to the world in a unique way. The information given in this manual provides a minimum of facts.

BEATRIX POTTER. (1886-1943) was a British author who wrote and illustrated children's stories. THE TALE OF PETER RABBITS is one of her books.

JOHN AMOS COMENIUS (1592-1670) was a Czeck educator who added illustrations to the educational textbook VISIBLE OBJECTS IN PICTURES, published in 1658. This book was the first educational textbook that contained pictures. Comenius believed that learning should be a pleasure and that pictures made a book more interesting.

THOMAS PAINE (1737-1809) was the writer of COMMON SENSE, a pamphlet published in 1776, that inspired the American colonists to fight for independence from English rule. Two quotations from COMMON SENSE are: "*These are the times that try men's souls.*" and "*Tyranny, like hell, is not easily conquered.*"

DOROTHEA LANGE. (1895-1965) was an American photographer who took pictures of people suffering through drought during the Great Depression. Newspapers and magazines published these pictures. These photographs helped create support for government relief programs for migrant workers.

RACHEL CARSON (1907-1964) was an American marine biologist and science writer. In 1962, her book, SILENT SPRING, stated that pesticides were contaminating plants, birds and animals. This contamination put all of us at risk. Her writings influenced governments to put restrictions on the use of pesticides.

Added discussion point:
"Which writers, illustrators and cartoonists, and photographers are influencing our country at this time?'

PA-7. Government Leaders p.18.

Beatrix - Netherlands	Catherine - Russia	Gandhi - India
Thatcher - England	Meir - Israel	Trudeau - Canada
Kalakaua - Hawaii	Frederick - Germany	DeGaulle - Frank
Thomas Jefferson - United States		

Write-in items 6+:
Permit much discussion of ideas when listing qualities of effective government leaders. If the students don't mention it, the instructor should say that qualities of governmental leaders may vary from culture to culture, and for different periods in time. A country seeking independence may

require a different type of leader than a country that already has independence. A country that is large with many types of topography and industry may require different leadership than a small country with one major industry.

Discuss: "People select their government leaders with their emotions - not their intelligence." Agree? Disagree?

PA-8. Community Service p.19.

Every member of society must contribute to that society if it is to survive. Community service or other non-paid services: 1) bring needed services to the community, and 2) provide a legacy that ives on in the lives of others in the community.

Encourage your students to identify, admire and imitate members of your community who provide community services to others. This is humanity at its best!

PA-9. People of Strong Conviction. p.20.

This group of persons is loved or hated. Learn of their lives and the causes they promoted. The information given here supplies only a few basic facts.

CLARA BARTON (1821-1912) devoted her life to better health services. Her greatest achievement was founding the Red Cross which brings medical supplies and needs to wounded and suffering people.

JANE ADDAMS (1860-1935) was a social worker and humanitarian. She established Hull House in Chicago where she bettered the living and working conditions for persons living in poverty conditions. Anyone receiving help from Hull House had to return services in some form. Hull House was not a handout, but a helping hand to those in need.

HARRIET TUBMAN (1821(?) - 1913) was a slave who ran away from her owner. The date of her birth cannot be verified - hence the questions mark after the birth date. Harriet helped more than 300 slaves escape into free territory by way of the Underground Railroad.

CARRY AMELIA NATION (1946-1911) was a crusader for abolition of all forms of alcohol. Her methods of opposition caused much concern. She also opposed tobacco and immodesty in dress.

MARTIN LUTHER KING. JR. (1929-1968) was a black civil rights leader who brought changes in social, political, and economic situations for blacks in the United States.

Study these people of strong conviction. Do not pass judgment on these people. A leadership training program is not a Sunday church lesson. The purpose of studying people of strong conviction is to inform students of how some persons promoted the causes in which they strongly believed.

PA-10. People of Achievement - Open Category. p.21.

Students select a category of leader. List names within that category and identify the achievements of each person names.

PA-11. List of People of Achievement. p.22.

This is a short list of leaders and their areas of leadership and achievement. It includes persons whose achievements touch the lives of many students. It does not include many persons whom your students may already know.

This list is provided to encourage students to read about others leaders and their achievements.

(LL) - Language of Leadership - instructor's manual

Objectives:
1. Bring attention to various forms of language that relates to leadership.
2. Teach public speaking.
3. Demonstrate, through group activities, that people differ in their interpretation of words, facial expressions, and viewpoints.
4. Grow in interest and respect for ideas of others.
5. Become more facile in the use of social phrases and etiquette.
6. Understand that body language and symbols are a form of condensed language.

General Comment

Activities in the Language of Leadership (LL) part develop the listening, speaking, and language skills needed for effective leadership. Each leadership training program should include some LL activities. Select the LL activities that will match your teaching abilities and style and the needs of your students.

LL-Language of Leadership

LL-1. Reading Facial Expressions. p.24.
People and cultures differ in interpretation of facial expressions. Leaders need to be aware of this. Leaders also must be able to read faces quickly and make decisions based on facial interpretation.

LL-2. Different Points of View. p.25.
Respond to the topic suggested in this activity. Permit much discussion.

LL-3. Considering Behavioral Choices. p.26.
Leaders must be versatile. Any given situation has many possible responses. Leaders assess a situation and then plan responses. Think of at three responses.

LL-4. Using Social Expressions. p.27.
The purpose of this page is to help students understand basic courtesy and societal expressions. Include a discussion on the importance of basic common courtesy in all human relations.

LL-5. Using Symbols. p.28.
Symbols are an abbreviated form of language. Symbols play a vital role in our rapid way of living. A symbol replaces many words. A symbol is immediately recognizable.

LEAD YOURSELF
BE A LEADER
LEAD OTHERS

LL-6. Written Communications. p.29.
Written communications could be a course - all by itself. But, because written communications are important to a leader, one page is added to the program. Some practice in letter writing and memo writing are encouraged.

LL-7. The Do's and Don'ts of Public Speaking p.30.
Read the lists. Some students like to demonstrate the "don'ts" !!

LL-8. Analyzing a Speech p.31.
Copy this page so that each student can analyze several speeches.

LL-9,10. Preparing a Speech: Information and Practice. p.32,33.
This is a simple format for a speech. It is a good format to teach basic speech preparation. Practice preparing a speech using the topic suggested or select a topic of your own.

LL-11. Understanding and Using Body Language p.34.
In recent years, we have become more aware of our use of body language. Students interested in knowing more about the topic should consult libraries for book on the subject.

LL-12. Tone of Voice; Statements of Persuasion. p.35.
Tone of voice is sometimes more important than the actual words spoken. Follow the directions on the page for several activities related to tone of voice and statements of persuasion.

LL-13. Public Reading as Part of Public Speaking p.36.
The leader who feels comfortable reading in public has an added skill. Follow the directions given. There is no substitute for practice. Reading in public is a highly polished useful skills.

Be careful not to drag out the leadership program or any particular activity. Rather do a few exercises and then move on.

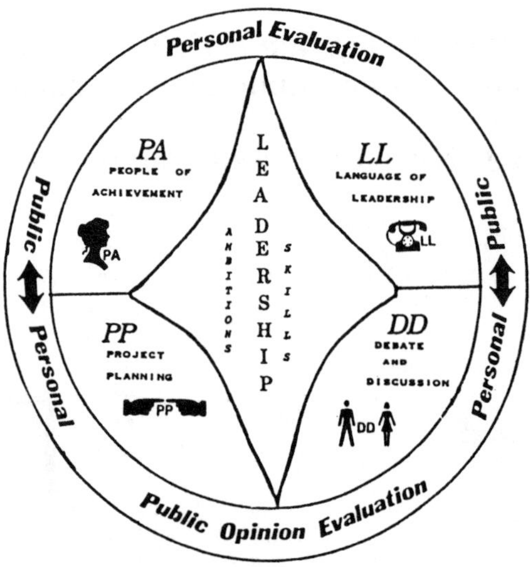

(PP) - Project Planning - instructor's manual

Objectives:
1. Study a system for planning and implementing a project..
2. Learn how to break a large project into smaller units.
3. Learn how and when to delegate responsibility.
4. Learn that personality style may influence the success or failure of a project.
5. Learn response options, such as: lead, follow, get out of the way.
6. Learn how to recognize and solve conflicts and/or problems.

General Comment

Activities in Project Planning (PP) provide information and skills in analysing a task, listing materials needed for a project, and other considerations necessary to put an idea into reality. Some PP activities must be included in a leadership training program. Instructors determine how much time will be spent in category of activities. Select the PP activities that will match your teaching abilities and the needs of the students.

PP-Project Planning

PP-1. Assign Person to Suitable Tasks. p.38.
People often respond in predictable patterns based on talent and abilities. A leader should delegate a task to a person who is capable of doing the task.

PP-2. Projects: Listing Supplies. p.39.
Students should ~~cross out~~ items not needed and (circle) those items needed for the task. Accept answers students can support. Students may add items needed but not listed.

PP-3. Listing Materials to Complete a Project. p.40.
Answers will vary. Accept answers students can support.

PP-4. Project Planning: Raising Fresh Vegetables. p.41.
Follow the directions.

Leadership Workshop

PP-5. Flowchart: Project Planning - Sequence of Events pp.42,43.
PP-6. Flowchart for Project Planning - Committees Required. pp.44,45.
Project planning is at the heart of organizing a project. Flowcharts are useful tools for organizing a project. The forms should be studied. Students develop their own plans.

When a group project is planned, make enough copies so that every person involved has a copy of the flowchart. This assures the person that he/she knows what task is expected and what tasks have been assigned to others. Put another copy on the bulletin board.

Much frustration and confusion can be avoided when flowcharts are used. It is worth the time and effort to master flowcharting a project.

PP-7. Group Dynamics: Problems. p.46.
PP-8. Group Dynamics: Consensus-Building. p.47
Accept all answers students can support.

PP-9. Lead, Follow, Get Out of the Way: Personal Choices. p.48.
PP-10. Worksheet for Lead, Follow, Get Out of the Way. pp. 49.
Students should understand that each decision is valid. Sometimes, it is better to get out of the way then to lead. Do not let anyone force you to take a position if you do not want to accept. If you elect to follow, then follow - don't try to take over.

PP-11. Troubleshooting. p.50.
A "troubleshooter" is a person who can assess a situation, see the problem, and suggest how to correct the problem(s).

√ Identify the project.
√ Identify the Problem.
√ Suggest at least 3 solutions.

Answers will vary.

(DD) - Debate & Discussion - instructor's manual

Objectives:

1. To share ideas, viewpoints and opinions.
2. To practice attentive listening and responding.
3. To develop an interest in multiple viewpoints.
4. To gain respect for ideas of others.
5. To learn and develop problem solving skills.
6. To learn how people persuade (or coerce) others.
7. To understand the opportunity of emotional moments.
8. To understand contemporary terms and concepts.

General Comment

Activities in Debate and Discussion (DD) develop habits, attitudes and skills to see issues from many perspectives. Problem solving skills and fact-finding are parts of debate and discussion. Instructors determine how much time will be spend on DD activities. Select the DD activities that will meet your teaching abilities and needs of your students.

DD-Debate and Discussion

DD-1. Group Sharing of Ideas and Techniques. p.52.

Participants in the leadership program should consider the questions listed here. Answers will vary considerably.

In Debate and Discussion, the purpose is to share ideas - not convert people to your viewpoint.

DD-2. Listening and Restatement of an Idea. p.53.

Listening and restating an idea is important in leadership. Some term this "reflective listening." Some suggestions are given. Accept any supported viewpoints.

1. I like big and expensive birthday gifts.
2. I like gym, recess and science classes.
3. Money doesn't buy everything.
4. People who speak different languages can understand art and music.
5. Jewelry makes the wearer feel good.
6. I prefer to eat where there is light.
7. People complain about the same things year after year.
8. I get tired when I have had an active full day.
9. He's a good salesman.

LEAD YOURSELF
BE A LEADER
LEAD OTHERS

10. New acquaintances provide new viewpoints.
11. Some games are for all ages.
12. Advertising influences purchasing decisions.
13. I want the glory of the athlete but not the self-discipline.
14. The fact that something happened once, does not mean it will happen again.
15. Shoes with worn holes and cracked soles are worn out.
16. Teachers get angry when a student doesn't do assignments for three days.

DD-3. Paraphrasing. p.54.

Leaders who use many cliches and idioms are often trying to bluff through a situation, or hope to persuade you by common expressions. *A good leader uses idioms with care.* Idioms and cliches, while sometimes a good tool, are not a substitute for exact language.

The explanations given here are suggested interpretations. Others may also be correct.

Don't count your chickens until they are hatched.
Eggs are not truly chickens until they are hatched and are clearly seen as healthy chickens.

He was caught red-handed.
To be "red-handed" was a murderer with blood still on the hands. To be caught red-handed can be to be discovered with evidence clearly seen.

A bird in the hand is worth two in the bush.
If you want to catch birds (or achieve goals), the bird (or goal) already caught (or achieved) is better than birds (goals) beyond reach.

This is like trying to find a needle in the haystack.
A haystack has millions of bits of dried hay, many about the size of a needle. To look for a needle in a haystack is to attempt what seems impossible.

Let sleeping dogs lie.
A dog, when sleeping, is not a threat. When it awakens, it may be a threat.

Let's settle this and bury the hatchet.
The hatchet, symbol of aggression, is put aside for negotiated agreement.

All that glitters is not gold.
Glittery things attract. There are attractive things besides gold, the symbol of wealth and power.

Slow and steady wins the race.
A person who works steadily is dependable and reliable.

You can't tell the book by its cover.
Sometimes external appearances are deceiving.

He speaks out of both sides of his mouth.
He says things that cannot be true because one statement contradicts another.

It happened out of the blue.
It happened without any warning.

It is raining cats and dogs.
The rain is a heavy downpour.

They fit like two peas in a pod.
They fit together or think alike.

Stop this monkey business.
Get at the task you are supposed to be doing. Stop doing silly things.

He was stopped cold.
He was quickly stopped before further actions could be taken.

Shape up or ship out.
Do as the group does, or leave the group.

Secure as a clam at high tide.
High tide means the clam is in water - where it wants to be.

This is bringing coals to Newcastle.
Newcastle has coal. There is no point bring more coal.

He bought a pig in a poke.
A "poke" is a pocket. Buying a pig in a poke is buying something you haven't seen.

A fool and his money are quickly parted.
A foolish person doesn't know how to wisely use money.

He's a chip off the old block.
The boy is like his father.

Better late than never.
It is better to come late than not to come at all.

This situation is a can of worms.
Worms in a can wiggle in all directions and are difficult to control.

Every cloud has a silver lining.
Many unpleasant situations can have good aspects or be changed into something that has value.

Happiness is its own reward.
To be happy or at peace is a reward, sometimes better than a reward of financial value.

Let bygones by bygones.
Forget what happened in the past and deal with the present.

The pen is mightier than the sword.
Written words impress people more strongly than do swords that try to kill opposers.

Don't build air castles in the sky.
A castle in the sky can never be useful.

DD-4. Island Survival. p.55.
There are many variations on this simple but challenging activity. Enjoy!

DD-5. Cooperation or Coercion? pp. 56, 57.
The leadership training program would not be valid or complete without a review of ways, fair and unfair, that people have of forcing cooperation. This is a delicate page -- delicate because it touches so near to people's fears and feelings. In another sense, it is a tough page that explains that people force cooperation in many ways.

Followers need to know these techniques so that a bully leader does not take advantage of them. Leaders need to know these techniques so that they can avoid them and rely on more fair means. Also, the leader needs to know these techniques because followers and hecklers use them to interfere with the work of the leader.

Be aware of these techniques. Students have a greater likelihood in resisting these techniques when they are aware of them. *Fore-warned is fore-armed!*

DD-6. Tolerance for Diversity. p.58
This is an awareness page. Let it be so.

DD-7. Emotional Moments. p.59.
A leader is not always appreciated, valued and cherished. Leaders are often the object of heated emotional outbursts. Let the group suggest responses of "B" - the leader. Caution students: *Is your solution helping or creating another problem?* Follow the directions on the page.

DD-8. Problem Recognition & Solution Guide. pp.60.
DD-9. Problem Solving. p.61.
Here are two methods of recognizing and solving problems. Teach methods of problem recognition and solving to all students. They are life-long skills.

DD-10. Spotlight on. . . . . p.62.
Give tribute to a person or event of choice.

DD-11. Risk! p.63.
There is much discussion about students "at risk" and business ventures being "risky business". Here is the opportunity for students to conceptualize "risk" - in words or graphics. *Give no directions other than the directions at the bottom of the page.* Then permit quiet time while participants respond. This activity can also be done with a single piece of paper - any paper. Just make sure every participant has the same type of paper. Share results with each other.

DD-12. General Concerns. p.64.
This looks like a simple page but it requires much effort. Share your examples with others. Leaders deal with all of the concepts listed here.

Teacher Helps - instructor's manual

Objectives:
1. To provide the teacher with additional suggestions that may be helpful.
2. To provide formal and informal leadership identification procedures.
3. To provide forms that save time for teachers.
4. To provide patterns: certificate, award and "buttons"..

Teacher Helps.

Leadership Instructional Model. p.66.
The components of leadership are People of Achievement (PA), Language of Leadership (LL), Project Planning (PP) and Debate and Discussion (DD). Surrounding all is Public and Personal Opinion Evaluation. Leadership is a continuous process.

Leadership Project - a Plan. p.67.
This planning form may help students plan or begin a leadership project. The form also provides a section to judge "results". Leadership projects may be successful because they achieved the desired goal. Or, projects are successful by what was learned even though the desired goal was not achieved.

Suggestions for Project Planning. p.68.
Suggested Problems for Problem Solving. p.69
These are suggestions - if you or your students need any.

Recognizing Leadership in Students. p.70.
This is an informal method of identifying students in leadership.

Roets Rating Scale for Leadership (RRSL). p.71.
This is a formal method of identifying students in leadership.
It is valid for ages 8-18. The following seven pages are:

Roets Rating Scale for Leadership (RRSL)

A Self-rating Identification Measure for Leadership for Ages 10-18.

Author: Lois Roets Ed.D.

GENERAL DESCRIPTION

THE ROETS RATING SCALE FOR LEADERSHIP (RRSL) is a self-rating scale for students grades 5-12. It is a measurement for students to rate themselves. It measures leadership (already active or in the daydream stage), ambition, and desires. Grades 5-12 may also be considered as ages 10-18.

HOW TO ADMINISTER THE RRSL

Students in grades 5-12, or ages 10-18, are asked to rate self on the 26 items listed in the RRSL. Students use a numerical code to rate self. The numerical self-rating code is: 1—almost always, 2—quite often, 3—sometimes, 4—not very often, 5—never.

Instructor tells the students:

"Students, today we will complete a self-rating scale. This self-rating scale will ask you to rate yourself. To rate yourself, means to give yourself a number. The numbers we will use are: (have on display or chalkboard): 1—almost always, 2—quite often, 3—sometimes, 4—not very often, 5—never. There are no right or wrong answers. You are asked to rate self as you see yourself. I may tell you what a word means, but I cannot give you a suggestion as to how you should rate yourself.

"Let's do an example. Using the 5-point rating scale, how would you rate yourself on these items:

______ *I like to read before I fall asleep at night.*

______ *I would like to be chosen to be part of a basketball team.*

______ *I am embarrassed when I give a wrong answer.*

Any questions?"

Be certain students understand how to rate self. When the self-rating process is understood, students should complete the scale as quickly as possible. Urge them to move ahead and give the rating that best describes self. Do not ponder too long on any one item.

HOW TO SCORE THE RRSL

Student scores are tabulated in this fashion:

Responses of 1 =3 points each, responses of 2 =2 points each, responses of 3 =1 point each. Total all points. Responses of 4 and 5 neither add nor subtract.

RATING SCALE FOR LEADERSHIP

A Self-rating Scale by Dr. Lois Roets

Completed Sample

Name *John Doe* Age *12* Grade *6* Date *10-86*

DIRECTIONS: Read each statement. Mark with the number of your choice.

1—almost always 2—quite often 3—sometimes 4—not very often 5—never

1 I have strong convictions about things.
1 When I believe in something, I work to promote it.
3 I listen to both sides of the issue before I make up my mind.
3 I have self-confidence.
2 I am able to say my opinions in public.
1 I usually am satisfied with the decisions I make.
2 When I am criticized for some action I have taken, I can usually go about my work.
2 I like to be in charge of events.
1 I am able to see what materials are needed to complete a project.
1 I am able to see the sequence of steps necessary to complete a project.
2 When I am convinced of something, I have courage to act for it.
3 I often lead in projects.
2 When I see somebody who is a leader, I think that I could do as well as that leader.
3 I can speak to persons in authority.
2 I have energy to complete projects that I am interested in completing.
1 I can understand the viewpoints of others.
2 I am willing to change my mind if new facts suggest that I should change my mind.
3 I get anxious and excited and am able to use this energy to complete a task.
3 I am able to work with many types of persons and personalities.
2 I usually understand the plot of a story or play or the main point in a conversation.
3 I am willing to try new experiences when these seem wise.
3 I know when to lead, to follow and to get out of the way.
1 I admire people who have achieved great things.
1 I dream of the day and time when I am able to lead myself or others to great accomplishment.
4 I feel at ease asking people for help or information.
2 I can be a "peacemaker" if I want to be.

Responses of 1 = 8 x3 = 24
Responses of 2 = 9 x2 = 18
Responses of 3 = 8 x1 = 8
total 50 pts

53rd percentile
5th stanine

Interpreting RRSL Scores

Using total scores, assign a percentile and stanine rank by consulting conversion table page

Using the RRSL Scores

Educators must determine which students should be offered leadership training. Some schools offer leadership training to anyone who wishes to take it. Other schools make leadership training a mandatory program for a specified subtotal of total student population. Other plans include using the RRSL percentile and stanine ranks to make these decisions:

— leadership training will be offered to all students scoring at or above the 40th percentile.

— leadership training will be offered to all students scoring at or above the 4th stanine.

— leadership training will be offered to top quartile (75th percentile or above and/or 3rd stanine or above).

— leadership training will be offered to those students scoring in the upper half (50th percentile or above and/or 5th stanine or above) **and** who have one other recommendation for leadership. Recommendation may come from self, teacher, peer, or parent.

Other plans may be equally effective.

What is being said is this: **Leadership Training should be a vital part of the enriched curriculum.** The ROETS RATING SCALE FOR LEADERSHIP (RRSL) is a valid and reliable measure for leadership. But the RRSL is not a perfect measure, nor is it the only leadership identification measure available. Do NOT interpret the scores on the RRSL as absolutes, as leadership measures are always improving. Also, the nature of leadership states that person's leadership abilities and ambitions can be stifled or nurtured.

ROETS RATING SCALE FOR LEADERSHIP

RAW SCORES CONVERTED TO PERCENTILE RANK AND STANINES

RAW SCORE	PERCENTILE	STANINE	RAW SCORE	PERCENTILE	STANINE	RAW SCORE	PERCENTILE	STANINE
78	99	9	52	59	5	26	6	2
77	99		51	57		25	5	
76	99		50	53		24	4	1
75	99		49	50		23	3	
74	99		48	46		22	3	
73	98		47	44		21	3	
72	98		46	41		20	3	
71	97		45	38	4	19	2	
70	96		44	36		18	2	
69	95	8	43	33		17	2	
68	94		42	30		16	1	
67	93		41	28		15	1	
66	91		40	25		14	1	
65	89		39	23	3	13	1	
64	88	7	38	21		12	1	
63	86		37	20		11	1	
62	84		36	18		10	1	
61	82		35	17		9	1	
60	80		34	15		8	1	
59	78		33	14		7	1	
58	75	6	32	12		6	1	
57	73		31	11	2	5	1	
56	70		30	10		4	1	
55	67		29	9		3	1	
54	64		28	8		2	1	
53	62		27	7		1	1	

RATING SCALE FOR LEADERSHIP

FREQUENCY DISTRIBUTION OF TEST SCORES N-1057

S-TOTAL STUDENT SCORE F-FREQUENCY

S F	S F	S F	S F	S F	S F	S F	S F
78-0	69-10	59-30	49-42	39-13	29-12	19-3	9-2
77-0	68-14	58-27	48-30	38-15	28- 8	18-4	8-0
76-1	67-21	57-16	47-30	37-15	27- 9	17-4	7-0
75-4	66-20	56-39	46-33	36-18	26- 8	16-1	6-0
74-7	65-16	55-28	45-20	35-16	25-11	15-0	5-0
73-7	64-11	54-30	44-22	34-15	24- 6	14-1	4-1
72-6	63-21	53-26	43-39	33-17	23- 8	13-0	3-0
71-9	62-22	52-24	42-25	32-13	22- 2	12-3	2-0
70-12	61-21	51-32	41-29	31-12	21- 2	11-1	1-0
	60-26	50-36	40-31	30-15	20- 3	10-2	

Median = 49

DISTRIBUTION FOR STANINE COMPUTATION N-1057

STANINE	PERCENT OF TOTAL	SCORE RANGE	NUMBER OF 1057 WHO SCORED IN THAT RANGE
9	4%	70-78	46
8	7%	65-69	81
7	12%	59-64	131
6	16%	53-58	166
5	22%	46-52	227
4	16%	40-45	166
3	12%	32-39	122
2	7%	25-31	75
1	4%	0-24	43

VALIDITY AND RELIABILITY OF

RATING SCALE FOR LEADERSHIP

The ROETS RATING SCALE FOR LEADERSHIP (RRSL) was administered to 1057 students in grades 5-12, living in continental United States. Chart 1 shows distribution of students completing the RRSL.

Chart 1.

DISTRIBUTION OF STUDENTS, GRADES 5-12 N - 1057

CITY STATE	TYPE OF SCHOOL		NUMBER OF STUDENTS		TOTAL
	PUBLIC	PRIVATE	FIRST STUDY	SECOND STUDY	
COLUMBUS, IND	●		18		18
LINWOOD, NJ	●		8		8
SANDUSKY, OHIO		□	58		58
LAKE CITY, SC		□	11		11
ADDISON, MAINE	●		1		1
MELBOURNE, FLORIDA	●		18	63	81
SAN FRANCISCO, CA		□	11		11
ANNA, ILLINOIS		□	9		9
WAYNESVILLE, OHIO	●		18		18
SPARTA, ILLINOIS		□	8		8
OAK GROVE, VIRGINIA	●		10		10
WEIRTON, WEST VIRGINIA		□	14	60	74
BOULDER, COLORADO	●		10		10
KINGWOOD, WEST VIRGINIA	●		7		7
SALUDA, S. CAROLINA	●		29		29
DAVIS, CALIFORNIA	●		31		31
BROOKINGS, OREGON	●		5		5
LEXINGTON, OKLAHOMA	●		6		6
READING, MASSACHUSETTS	●		11		11
BAYONNE, NEW JERSEY	●		8		8
CHICAGO CITY, MINN	●		25		25
MT. CLEMENS, MICHIGAN	●		17		17
INDIANAPOLIS, IND.	●		5		5
COLUMBUS, OHIO		□	11		11
NEW SHARON, IOWA	●		77	29	106
ROSEMONT, MINNESOTA	●			39	39
OLATHE, KS FIRST SCHOOL	●			36	36
OLATHE, KS SECOND SCHOOL	●			29	29
OAKDALE, CONNECTICUT	●			27	27
DEL VALLE, TEXAS	●			50	50
HOBBS, NEW MEXICO	●			33	33
EVARTS, KENTUCKY	●			54	54
WINDSOR, VERMONT	●			10	10
SULLY, IOWA	●			56	56
CINCINNATI, OHIO	●			8	8
DOUGLAS, WYOMING	●			9	9
PEACH TREE, GEORGIA	●			50	50
SALT LAKE CITY, UTAH	●			78	78
TOTALS	31	7	426	631	1057

Students in grades 5-12 were asked to complete the RRSL. Chart 2 shows grade distribution of 1057 Ss who took part in the validation and reliability studies.

Chart 2. GRADE DISTRIBUTION OF STUDENTS N-1057

GRADE 5	GRADE 6	GRADE 7	GRADE 8	GRADE 9	GRADE 10	GRADE 11	GRADE 12
159	175	163	120	89	89	106	156

Chart 3 lists the mean, standard deviation, and variance for scores on the RRSL for 1057 Ss in grades 5-12.

Chart 3

MEAN, STANDARD DEVIATION, VARIANCE FOR RRSL N-1057

MEAN	STANDARD DEVIATION	VARIANCE
48	13	174.010

VALIDITY OF ROETS RATING SCALE FOR LEADERSHIP (RRSL)

Validity for the ROETS RATING SCALE FOR LEADERSHIP was established with 631 Ss of 1057 Ss. Students completed the RRSL and two other leadership identification measures. In addition to the RRSL, students completed the "Leadership" portion of SCALES FOR RATING BEHAVIORAL CHARACTERISTICS OF SUPERIOR STUDENTS (SRBCSS) by Renzulli, White, Smith, Callahan, Hart (Creative Learning Press, PO Box 320, Mansfield Center, CT 06259, copyright, 1976) and CHECKLIST FOR LEADERSHIP assembled by Roger Taylor and a group of Illinois teachers.

Correlation between RRSL and "Leadership" portion of SCALES FOR RATING BEHAVIORAL CHARACTERISTICS OF SUPERIOR STUDENTS, 631 Ss,= +.71

Correlation between RRSL and Checklist for Leadership (R. Taylor et al), 631 Ss, = +.77

Correlation between CHECKLIST FOR LEADERSHIP (R. Taylor et al) and "Leadership" portion (SRBCSS, Renzulli et al), based on 333 Ss subsample of 631, is + .63.

Of the 631 Ss, 137 Ss were asked to complete the "Motivation" and "Creativity" portions of SRBCSS. This was requested as a measure to see if items on the LEADERSHIP measures may also be closely related to creativity and motivation. It seemed logical to believe that leaders are also creative and motivated persons. The correlations, listed on Chart 4, add credibility to the assumption that leaders are creative and motivated. However, a leader has unique qualities, in addition to being creative and motivated.

Note: The letter "r" refers to "correlation."

Chart 4

CORRELATIONS BETWEEN LEADERSHIP, CREATIVITY, MOTIVATION N-137

	LEADERSHIP (ROETS) & CREATIVITY	LEADERSHIP (RENZULLI) & CREATIVITY
r	+.40	+.35
	LEADERSHIP (ROETS) & MOVITATION	LEADERSHIP (RENZULLI) & MOTIVATION
r	+.55	+.38

RELIABILITY OF ROETS RATING SCALE FOR LEADERSHIP (RRSL)

Reliability of the RRSL was established through Spearman-Brown Split Halves Prophecy formula.* This approach to reliability is used when only one form of a test is available. The items on the test (scale) are divided into two half tests, called "split halves." The correlation between total scores on the two halves is lower than the correlation between two complete test forms. The reliability of the entire test can, however, be estimated from the correlation between the half tests. The Spearman-Brown Prophecy formula is as follows:

Let R = correlation between two comparable test forms
Let r = correlation between two half tests

$$\text{Then } R = \frac{2r}{1+r}$$

Using the above formula, the ROETS RATING SCALE FOR LEADERSHIP, based on split halves of 631 Ss, grades 5-12, computes a reliability correlation of + .85.

It was of interest to compute reliability correlation of the "Leadership" portion of SRBCSS since that identification measure is more widely used than the RRSL. Reliability correlation of "leadership" portion of SRBCSS, based on Spearman-Brown Prophecy formula applied to scores of 631 Ss, is + .59.

CONCLUSION

The ROETS RATING SCALE FOR LEADERSHIP is a valid and reliable measure for leadership ability for students grades 5-12.

**ELEMENTARY STATISTICAL METHODS by Walker and Lev, page 233. Holt, Rinehart, Winston. Copyright, 1969.*

Readings: Books, Magazine, Newspapers. pp.72,73.
Some students or teachers like to compile or keep records of readings. These two record sheets may help.

Student Evaluation for the Leadership Program. p.74.
Students who complete a short or extended course in leadership training should do some form of evaluation. This evaluation form follows the contents. You may design your own also.

Certificate and Award. p.75.
Issue one or both - as needed to encourage leadership in students.

There are many good computer programs that will generate more personalized awards and recognitions. It could be a project for a young leader to locate the software, learn how to use it, and be in charge of printing/awarding recognitions.

Leadership Button Patterns. pp.76,77.
Simple patterns. Use them. Or, use computer software to create your own buttons, stickers or promotions. Self-adhesive labels - including several size circles - are available from office supply companies. School offices have such catalogs. Be creative. But, teachers, don't you do the work. Let students do it.

Notes. p. 78

Appendices

Leadership Workshop

Appendix A

Establishing a LEADERSHIP Program in your school

Step One: Mental conviction that leadership training should be offered.

Convictions arise from:

- √ personal observation of students who need more opportunities to express leadership,
- √ observation of students who feel that they have no control over their own life,
- √ teachers/parents think students would benefit from leadership opportunities.
- √ concern for special populations to strengthen leadership of individuals and/or group.

Step Two: Select a Leadership Program that meets the needs of students and instructional style of the instructor.

Step Three: Secure Permissions to offer Leadership classes.

Step Four: In-service Key People.

In-service should include: content of the leadership program, selection processes for participation, scheduling information, and desired outcomes from the program. Key people are administrators, groups of teachers, parents and students.

Step Five: Initiate selection process for participants.

See suggestions page 103.

Step Six: Leadership training program is held for first group of students.

Use as the author designed it or modify to meet your particular needs.

Classes are held during regular class time, on Saturdays, with total classes, at a given time slot for 4 weeks such as a pull-out program or regularly scheduled enrichment class, or other agreed-upon schedule.

Step Seven: Individual and group projects are completed.

Projects are self-selected and are completed individually or in a small group. Every project should be reviewed with at least one person who will reinforce student efforts. When appropriate, the projects should be shared with other students, faculty, school board and the community.

Step Eight: Evaluate the Program.

Evaluation is completed by students who took the program and others persons wishing to voice opinions relative to content, selection process, scheduling and outcomes of the leadership training program.

See also part 5 of page 67, bottom of page 70, or Evaluation page 74.

Step Nine: Adjust the Program and Plan for the Future.

Adjust the program relative to suggestions given in step seven.
Publicize the dates and times for the next leadership training session.

Step Ten: Maintain contact with students who completed the course.

Appendix B

Leadership Identification & Procedures

I. Standardized measure for identifying leadership developed by L. Roets is the self-rating scale for Grades 5-12: **Roets Rating Scale for Leadership** (RRSL).

- RRSL is on page 70 with instructions on using it on pp. 92-99.

A. Use the RRSL as a standardized measure.
Follow the directions and offer leadership classes and opportunities to students ranking in the upper quartile or third of the class/group/school. Or offer leadership opportunities for students ranking at stanines 7,8,or 9.

B. Use the RRSL as a non-standardized measure.
Complete the RRSL in class. Discuss. Students self select after completing the RRSL. Students who were interested in items on the scale may also be interested in taking the leadership class.

II. Non-Standardized procedures for identifying leadership ability.

A. Subjective recommendations.

***Subjective recommendations** are based on:*
A) committee-agreed definition or description of leadership behaviors & characteristics,
B) individual's definition of leadership behaviors & characteristics,,
C) individual's determination that a student needs more opportunities to lead self and/or others.

1. Peer Recommendation. - *complete a form, register on list...*
2. Self-recommendation. - *complete a form, register...*
3. Teacher recommendation - direct and/or indirect:

    a. Direct: *complete a form, register name...*
    Caution: teachers may recommend "teacher-pleasers" or "students who are good performers after someone tells them what to do".

    b. Indirect: *suggest to a student that he/she might like a leadership classes and opportunities.*

4. Parent recommendations. - *complete a form, register a name...*

B. "Register yourself and bring a friend"

C. Entire class is offered some leadership activities and then student self-selects to continue other activities.

D. Performance review panel. Observe or review what a person has done that shows leadership.

☞ See pages 70 & 79 for additional suggestions.

Appendix C

Additions to the Basic Leadership Training Program: Additions for the Four Instructional Components of Leadership: A Skills Training Program

People of Achievement (PA)

1. Community Service
   - A. List 5 persons in your community who have given time to improve the community. List the name and area of contribution. Interview one person.
   - B. List areas of improvement for your community.

2. A tolerance for diversity.
   - *A. Examples of achievers who were different or who helped others accept diversity.*

3. Analyzing effective leadership.

   Some factors that must be present are:
   - a. Support of the majority
   - b. Issue must be in agreement with the current value system.
   - c. The "right time" in the "right place"
   - d. Risk-taking at the right moment.

     e.g. Yeltsin standing on the Soviet tank calling for denunciation of the coup and calling for a boycott of the curfew imposed by the organizers of the coup.
   - e. A vision of the future.
   - f. Know when to "hang in there" and when to regroup of give up.

Language of Leadership (LL)

1. A need for civility - defining it, using it, as a foundation for building partnerships.
2. Selling your ideas.

   Suggestion: Finding out what your listeners want to hear or are interested in and then modeling you approach to match that.

Project Planning (PP)

1. Committee selection - how to select, who to put in charge
2. Consensus building -

Debate and Discussion (DD)

1. Conflict identification / containment/ resolution.
2. Open-mindedness - To what degree is that possible?
3. Willingness to compromise
4. Accepting ambiguity.

Adapting Basic LEADERSHIP Training Program for Special Populations

Identify the Population to be Served

Identify the special population you wish to serve.

1. Identify the population by age, grade, sex, geographic group or other factors that define the group as a "special population."
2. Identify the special leadership needs of the group.
3. Identify the group's strengths and special interests.
4. Identify cultural "acceptables" and "unacceptables"

Accept or Modify Basic LEADERSHIP TRAINING PROGRAM

Review the basic LEADERSHIP training program with a select group of individuals who represent the special population. This group should include : parents, educators, civic members and maybe students nd religious leaders.

From the review of the basic LEADERSHIP program, the activities will be judged appropriate to the special population or not appropriate. If judged appropriate, no further adaptation need be made. If judged inappropriate, eliminate or adjust the activity.

Leadership Activities that are Frequently Modified for Special Populations

Most special populations want to adjust the PEOPLE OF ACHIEVEMENT portion so that the people of achievement studied reflect the achievers from their own special population.

Other activities frequently adjusted are the sections on PROBLEM SOLVING, BEHAVIORAL OPTIONS, USING SOCIAL EXPRESSIONS, BODY LANGUAGE, PERSUASION and TONES OF VOICE.

Specific Suggestions for Modifying the Leadership Training Program

(PA) PEOPLE OF ACHIEVEMENT

The PA portion of LEADERSHIP calls attention to achievers who achieved what they set out to do. These achievers may have achieved results in a socially acceptable or unacceptable way. The point to be considered is this: *the achiever or leader is considered successful if the goal is reached.* It is the group or society at large that passes judgment on the moral rightness or wrongness of the achieved goal. The committee that reviewed the basic LEADERSHIP training program should select which people of achievement are most suitable for study with any given special population.

Study people of achievers who served or came from the special population currently participating in the leadership training program. The achievers studied should come from various areas of achievement that have lasting impact upon the special population. Therefore, achievers studied should come from writers or social leaders who shaped public sentiment, lawmakers or rulers who established and enforced laws, religious leaders who shaped the philosophy of life espoused by a large portion of the special population, and inventors who bettered the world.

(LL) LANGUAGE OF LEADERSHIP

The committee that reviewed the basic LEADERSHIP training program should select which Language of Leadership (LL) activities are most suitable for study with any given special population. Activities that may need adjusting are:

READING FACIAL EXPRESSIONS

Some special populations are permitted free facial expressions without fear of censorship. Other groups are not. Select facial expressions for "reading" that will help the participants in the leadership training session to understand the great importance of reading facial expressions.

USING SOCIAL EXPRESSIONS

Make certain the acceptable behaviors of the special population and acceptable behaviors of the majority are clearly understood.

CONSIDERING BEHAVIORAL OPTIONS

You may wish to write plays and situations that concern the special population.

SYMBOLS and BODY LANGUAGE

Include symbols and body language that have a lot of meaning for the special population. Are the meanings the same as for the rest of the population? What problems arise when a special population's body language or symbols contradict the value system of the rest of society? These are issues that must be considered.

TONE OF VOICE

The pitch and tone of voice are often more important than the words spoken. In some languages, the pitch of the spoken word indicates the meaning of the word. What problems does this present for communicating and understanding the population as a whole?

(PP) PROJECT PLANNING

The committee that reviewed the basic LEADERSHIP TRAINING PROGRAM should select which Project Planning (PP) activities are most suitable for study with any given special population.

The activity that may need adjusting is Troubleshooting Solutions to Problems. Select problems that relate to those encountered by the special population. Problem solving is an essential skill in project planning and completion.

(DD) DEBATE & DISCUSSION

The committee that reviewed the basic LEADERSHIP training program should select which Debate and Discussion (DD) activities are most suitable for study with the special population. The activities that may need adjusting are Paraphrasing and Persuasion Techniques.

Paraphrasing is the practice of taking a commonly understood expression, such as "Haste Makes Waste", and putting it into other words. Use expressions common to the special population.

Persuasion (coercion) techniques are often used by special population and used upon special populations. *Everyone must recognize what the techniques are and how to resist them.* Some common techniques are: threat of punishment, the unknown, or retaliation; appeal to a person's generosity, ambition, or friendship; impose a sense of guilt; divide loyalty; or undermine self-confidence and courage. The special population taking the leadership training program must determine what techniques are effective for them and what techniques undermine the happiness of the group.

Conclusion

Leadership is a dual concept: *"Lead Yourself; Lead Others."*

Special populations require leadership training programs which help them understand the majority of the population and the special strengths that come with being a member of a special population. To achieve this, the basic LEADERSHIP TRAINING PROGRAM should be adapted to meet the needs of special populations.

Pitfalls that Interfere with Successful Student Leadership Programs

1. Lack of support from peers.
   Teachers - lack of support from other teachers or administrators.
   Students - students make fun of students who are active leaders.

2. Careless selection of participants for the first session.
   The first group is very important because it sets the tone for other groups.

3. Lack of mentors or "encouragers" for students completing leadership projects.

4. Failure to adjust the program for each group taking the leadership program.

5. Lack of scheduled time for leadership training program.
   Leadership training programs needs time & space.

6. Discouragement because of lack of time, support or energy to keep things going - <u>leadership</u> being one of many things that must keep going.

7. Failure to follow-up the leadership program and the leadership projects.
   Follow-up is important to solidify the value of the program.
   Follow-up should be between the group leader and the students, and the students with each other.
   Leadership projects require support and should be reviewed with appropriate audiences.

LEAD YOURSELF
LEAD OTHERS

Appendix F

Record of Students Recognized for Leadership

✳ Student Name ______________________________ Date ____________

Leadership____

____

✾ Student Name ______________________________ Date ____________

Leadership____

____

▲ Student Name ______________________________ Date ____________

Leadership____

____

✏ Student Name ______________________________ Date ____________

Leadership____

____

✳ Student Name ______________________________ Date ____________

Leadership____

____

★ Student Name ______________________________ Date ____________

Leadership____

____

Appendix G

Record of Leadership Projects

Leadership project____

____

____.

Student Names ____.

Date ______________

Leadership project____

____

____.

Student Names ____.

Date ______________

Leadership project____

____

____.

Student Names ____.

Date ______________

Leadership project____

____

____.

Student Names ____.

Date ______________

110

Appendix G

Record of Leadership Projects

Leadership project____

____

____ .

Student Names ______________________________________.

Date ________________

Leadership project____

____

____ .

Student Names ______________________________________.

Date ________________

Leadership project____

____

____ .

Student Names ______________________________________.

Date ________________

Leadership project____

____

____ .

Student Names ______________________________________.

Date ________________

111

A Call for Leaders and Leadership

- **Entrepreneurs** who will create products and processes that will enable us to keep a roof over our head, bread on our table, contribute to civilization, and leave a legacy for our children.
- **Philosophers** who remind us how slowly human progress is made and how people who are fundamentally the same differ profoundly in how that sameness is expressed.
- **Moralists** who will help us integrate the security of dogma with the necessity of adaptation.
- **Comedians** who help us keep a sense of perspective and humor in a humorless situation.
- **Artists** who help us see the world with clearer understanding.
- **Cartoonists** whose perceptions help us understand events.
- **Optimistic Altruistic Politicians** who propose solutions to our problems even though few of their ideas are accepted.
- **Parents and Elders** who care about the next generation and the world left for them.
- **Children** who learn the current wisdom of the world and then selectively adopt and adapt that wisdom.
- **Writers** of fiction & nonfiction who have important messages and lure us to hear or read those messages.
- **Musicians** who compose and perform music that touches our souls and inspires us to be better than we thought we could be.
- **Public Service People** (police officers, teachers, doctors, lawyers, clergy, social workers, counselors, ...) who remember that they chose those professions to help people become independent, confident, competent, lifelong learners and contributors to society.

⋆ **You** - only **you** can add to the world your unique leadership.

ISBN: 0-911943-52-8 *(8th edition - 1997)*